Financial Reporting and the Evaluation of Solvency

Quoth the Banker, "Watch Cash Flow"

Once upon a midnight dreary as I pondered weak and weary
Over many a quaint and curious volume of accounting lore,
Seeking gimmicks (without scruple) to squeeze through
   some new tax loophole,
Suddenly I heard a knock upon my door,
     Only this, and nothing more.

Then I felt a queasy tingling and I heard the cash a-jingling
As a fearsome banker entered whom I'd often seen before.
His face was money-green and in his eyes there could be seen
Dollar-signs that seemed to glitter as he reckoned up the score.
   "Cash flow," the banker said, and nothing more.

I had always thought it fine to show a jet black bottom line,
But the banker sounded a resounding, "No,
Your receivables are high, mounting upward toward the sky;
Write-offs loom. What matters is cash flow."
   He repeated, "Watch cash flow."

Then I tried to tell the story of our lovely inventory
Which, though large, is full of most delightful stuff.
But the banker saw its growth, and with a mighty oath
He waved his arms and shouted, "Stop! Enough!
   Pay the interest, and don't give me any guff!"

Next I looked for non-cash items which could add ad infinitum
To replace the ever-outward flow of cash,
But to keep my statement black I'd held depreciation back,
And my banker said that I'd done something rash.
    He quivered, and his teeth began to gnash.

When I asked him for a loan, he responded, with a groan,
That the interest rate would be just prime plus eight,
And to guarantee my purity he'd insist on some security—
All my assets plus the scalp upon my pate.
    Only this, a standard rate.

Though my bottom line is black, I am flat upon my back,
My cash flows out and customers pay slow.
The growth of my receivables is almost unbelievable;
The result is certain—unremitting woe!
And I hear the banker utter an ominous low mutter,
    "Watch cash flow."

———Herbert S. Bailey, Jr.

Reprinted from *Publishers Weekly*, January 13, 1975, published by R. R. Bowker Company. Copyright © 1975 by Xerox Corporation.

3 | ACCOUNTING RESEARCH MONOGRAPH

Financial Reporting and the Evaluation of Solvency

by Loyd C. Heath, Ph.D.
Associate Professor of Accounting
University of Washington

American Institute of Certified Public Accountants
1211 Avenue of the Americas   New York, N.Y. 10036

Copyright © 1978 by the
American Institute of Certified Public Accountants, Inc.
1211 Avenue of the Americas
New York, N.Y. 10036
First Impression 1978

Publication of this study by the American Institute of Certified Public Accountants does not in any way constitute official endorsement or approval of the conclusions reached or the opinions expressed.

Contents

Foreword xi

Preface xiii

1 **"Though My Bottom Line Is Black, I Am Flat Upon My Back"** 1
   Profitability and Solvency 1
   Solvency Distinguished From Liquidity and Bankruptcy 2
   Importance of Solvency 2
   Information Needed to Evaluate Solvency 3
   Emphasis on Profitability 4
   Scope and Objectives of This Study 7
   Sources of Information 8
   Recommendations 8

2 **The Evaluation of Solvency** 11
   Early Credit Analysis 11
   Changing Emphasis in Credit Analysis 15
   Current Views of Credit Analysis 16
      Cash Flows 16
      Financial Position 19
   Financial Flexibility 20
      Borrowing Capacity 21
      Asset Disposability 21
      Cost Flexibility 23
      Dividend Flexibility 23
      Stock Flexibility 23
   Conclusion 23

3 **Historical Development of Balance Sheet Classification Practice** 25
   Origin and Influence of Asset Classification Concepts 26
      Origin in Economics 26
      Double-Account Balance Sheet 26
      Early Court Decisions 27
      Asset Valuation Practices 28

Evolution of Classification in American Practice   30
   Bankers' Influence on Early U.S. Practice   30
   Conflicting Early Practice   32
   Controversy in Accounting Literature   35
   Waning Influence of Bankers   36
Development of ARB No. 30   38
   Herrick's Views   39
   Opposition to Herrick   40
   The Compromise   41

4 Evaluation of Current-Noncurrent Classification Principles and Practices   43
Accounting Research Bulletin No. 30   44
   Faulty Definitions   44
   Current assets   44
   Current liabilities   47
   Itemized lists   49
   Evaluation of Underlying Concepts   51
   Basic concepts of classification   51
   Fixed and circulating capital   53
   Operating cycle   56
Usefulness of Current Practice   57
   Attribute Disclosure   58
   Prediction of Financial Failure   62
   Calculation Convenience   67
Summary and Conclusions   68

5 An Alternative to Current-Noncurrent Classification   71
Underlying Rationale of Recommended Changes   71
Recommendation   75
   Supplemental Information   75
   Classification of Liabilities   76
   Arrangement of Assets   78
Illustration and Discussion of Recommended Presentation   79
   Presentation of Assets   81
   Receivables   81
   Marketable securities   81
   Inventories   82
   Presentation of Liabilities   83
   Trend to More Disclosure   85
Summary and Implications of Recommendations   85

6 Funds Statements: Underlying Issues 87
   Historical Development of Funds Statements   87
      Where Got-Where Gone Statements   88
      Statement of Changes in Working Capital   88
      Alternatives to Changes in Working Capital   90
      Authoritative Pronouncements on Funds Statements   92
   Role of Funds Statements in Financial Reporting   96
      Business Activities and Financial Statements   96
      Limitations of Financial Statements   98
      Unrealistic and Worthless Objectives   98
   Evaluation of Current Practice   103
      Stated Objectives   103
      Implicit Objectives   104
   Conclusions   106

7 Recommended Replacements for the Statement of Changes in Financial Position 109
   Statement of Cash Receipts and Payments   109
      General Rationale   110
      Users' Views   114
      Accountants' Views   119
      Illustration of Recommended Statement of Cash Receipts and Payments   123
         Cash receipts and payments only   124
         Separate schedule of operations   124
         Cash provided by operations   124
         Operating vs. nonoperating activities   129
   Statement of Financing Activities   130
      General Rationale   130
      Illustration of Statement of Financing Activities   131
         Two types of financing   132
         Construction of the statement   132
   Statement of Investing Activities   134
   Conclusions   134

8 "Watch Cash Flow" 137
   Solvency Decision Models   137
   Awareness of Solvency Issues   139
      Rising Prices   140
      Consolidated Statements   140
      Pension Accounting   142
   Conclusion   142

Bibliography 145

Foreword

This is the third in the series of accounting research monographs that the Institute publishes to stimulate study and discussion of significant accounting problems. This study differs from other studies the Institute has published in that it deals with problems in financial reporting that the profession has not recognized and whose solution the profession is therefore not seeking. The author contends that the profession has overlooked or forgotten those problems—problems related to solvency—and that the accounting treatment of a number of issues has thereby suffered. He recommends significant changes in financial statement presentation to overcome shortcomings he feels have developed because solvency has not been given proper attention.

Proposals for changes in financial accounting related to profitability and valuation have become more insistent in recent years, and they are under study by the Financial Accounting Standards Board in its conceptual framework project. In that project, the board will also be studying issues in presentation, so the recommendations of this study concerning presentations are timely. The considerable changes in ingrained practices related to solvency recommended by this study should receive a sympathetic hearing when changes related to profitability are being considered. I commend this study to all those concerned with the improvement of financial reporting.

New York, N.Y.   PAUL ROSENFIELD
July, 1978   *Director, Accounting Standards*

Preface

This study is an outgrowth of a study of the accounting concept of working capital I was asked to undertake for the AICPA Accounting Principles Board before its functions were assumed by the Financial Accounting Standards Board. In the words of the APB planning subcommittee, that study was to deal with questions such as "Why do we have a working capital concept? How did it develop? What are we trying to do with it?"

Shortly after undertaking the working capital study, it became apparent that the main reason working capital classification was in such a confused state and that a research study of the subject was necessary was that accounting writers and policymakers had been asking the wrong question for many years. They had been asking how assets and liabilities should be classified so that the "true" amount of a company's working capital would be revealed instead of asking how classification of assets and liabilities as current and noncurrent provides information useful in evaluating a company's solvency. Once that broader question was raised, however, it led to even broader and more fundamental questions, such as what types of information are needed to evaluate a company's solvency and how can that information be best communicated to financial statement users. And, once those questions were raised, it was no longer feasible to limit the scope of the study to working capital classification alone because that practice had to be evaluated in the context of alternative methods of reporting information useful in solvency evaluation. Consequently, what was originally seen as a study of rather limited scope evolved into a much broader study of what I believe is one of the two major issues in financial reporting.

Many individuals and several organizations provided both direct and indirect help during the course of this study, and I would like to express my appreciation to them. Some of the most important indirect help in the form of providing an atmosphere conducive to undertaking a long-term project of this type came, in general, from the Graduate School of Business Administration at the University of

Washington and, in particular, from my department chairman, Professor Gerhard G. Mueller. Other important help in the form of financial assistance came from the American Institute of Certified Public Accountants, the Price Waterhouse Foundation, and the Accounting Development Fund at the University of Washington.

Many persons provided direct and invaluable help in the form of suggestions, comments, and criticism that improved the work significantly. Undoubtedly the most important came from Reed K. Storey, formerly director of accounting research of the AICPA (currently assistant director, research and technical activities, FASB) and from Paul Rosenfield, director, and Thomas W. McRae, manager, both of the AICPA Accounting Standards Division. Other important contributions were made by Professors Desmond McComb of the University of Southampton and Naomi Tsumagari of the University of Tokyo, members of the AICPA Project Advisory Committee on Working Capital (including particularly Robert P. Burns, chairman), members of the Northwest Accounting Research Group, and CPAs, lawyers, bankers, and financial analysts interviewed during the course of the study. My acknowledgment of these sources should not, of course, be construed as evidence of their concurrence with either the conclusions of this study or the reasoning underlying those conclusions.

Seattle, Washington LOYD C. HEATH
August, 1978

1

"Though My Bottom Line Is Black, I Am Flat Upon My Back"

The management of a business enterprise must be concerned with two broad objectives: (1) to operate the business profitably and (2) to maintain its solvency. *Profitability* refers to a company's ability to increase its wealth. *Solvency* refers to its ability to pay its debts when due.

Profitability and Solvency

Profitability and solvency are clearly related. Long-run solvency depends on long-run profitability. No method of obtaining money to pay debts will be available in the long run to an enterprise that is not profitable. In the short run, however, profitability and solvency do not necessarily go together. A profitable enterprise in need of cash to finance increasing receivables, inventory, and plant may tie itself to an unrealistic debt repayment schedule that results in its insolvency. On the other hand, an unprofitable enterprise may remain solvent for years because its cash collections continue to exceed its required cash payments.

Solvency Distinguished From Liquidity and Bankruptcy

Liquidity is closely related to solvency. The term *liquidity* is often used in at least two different ways. First, it is used to describe the nature of a company's asset holdings, that is, their "nearness" to cash in some (often unspecified) sense or, as one writer terms it, their "cash propinquity."[1] Second, it is used to describe some relationship between a company's liquid assets and its short-term liabilities. Both of these concepts of liquidity, however, are narrower than the concept of solvency as that term is used in this study. Both are balance sheet oriented. The nature of a company's assets and the relationship between its assets and its short-term liabilities are relevant in evaluating solvency, but solvency does not depend solely, perhaps not even primarily, on a company's recorded assets and liabilities; it depends on its ability to raise cash by whatever means available to it in relation to its need for cash. Although liquidity is sometimes used as a synonym for the broader concept of solvency, the term "liquidity" is avoided in this study wherever possible because it is so often used to refer only to asset characteristics and asset and liability structure.

Bankruptcy is related to insolvency, but the terms should be distinguished. *Bankruptcy* is the legal recognition of a state of insolvency. It describes the state of a company that has petitioned for, or been forced by its creditors to resort to, legal procedures to protect the right of creditors in a court-supervised reorganization or liquidation.

Importance of Solvency

Investors and creditors, the primary users of general purpose financial statements, need to evaluate the solvency as well as the profitability of companies in which they have an interest. Creditors are obviously concerned with solvency. In fact, evaluation of solvency is often referred to as *credit analysis*, although that term should not be taken to mean that creditors are the only parties interested in a company's solvency or even that creditors are more interested in solvency than other financial statement users. If a company becomes insolvent, equity investors are likely to lose even more than creditors, because creditors' rights are senior to those of stockholders in bankruptcy and reorganization proceedings. Even if a company never

---

1. F. W. Mueller, Jr., "Corporate Working Capital and Liquidity," *Journal of Business*, 26, no. 3 (July, 1953): 165.

reaches the point of insolvency, the mere threat or suspicion of insolvency is likely to result in losses to stockholders. The more obvious consequences are that the market value of their shares is likely to decline and that increased costs of borrowing money will tend to reduce profits. But less obvious consequences may be just as serious. Even if there is no imminent threat of insolvency, a company that is short of cash will have to pass up profitable investment opportunities and restrict cash payments in ways that are likely to affect long-run profitability.

Other financial statement users are also concerned with a company's solvency. Employees, suppliers, and customers are concerned because loss of solvency usually means loss of jobs, loss of customers, and disruption of sources of supply. The U.S. government's guarantee of loans to Lockheed Corporation several years ago illustrates society's concern over the solvency of at least one major corporation.

Information Needed to Evaluate Solvency

The information needed to evaluate solvency is different from that needed to evaluate profitability. Solvency is a money or cash phenomenon. A solvent company is one with adequate cash to pay its debts; an insolvent company is one with inadequate cash. Evaluating solvency is basically a problem of evaluating the risk that a company will not be able to raise enough cash before its debts must be paid. Any information that provides insight into the amounts, timing, and uncertainty of a company's future cash receipts and payments is, therefore, relevant in evaluating its solvency. Also, since companies operate in a world of uncertainty in which future events can only be estimated, a company's ability to control its cash receipts and payments to bring cash receipts into balance with required cash payments is also relevant.[2]

Cash receipts and payments are also relevant in evaluating a company's profitability, but in a different way. The timing of a company's receipts and payments is irrelevant in the measurement of income except insofar as timing affects the amounts at which assets and liabilities are recorded. The sale of an item for $10,000 cash and the sale of that same item for a $10,000 note receivable due in five

---

2. A company's ability to control its cash receipts and payments is referred to as its financial flexibility, which is discussed more fully in chapter 2.

years with interest at 10 percent are regarded as equivalent transactions in evaluating profitability. They are not equivalent, however, in evaluating solvency because the timing of the cash receipts differs greatly in the two cases. The *timing* of future cash receipts and payments is the sine qua non of solvency evaluation and the heart of the distinction between issues of solvency reporting and profitability reporting.

Emphasis on Profitability

During the first three decades of this century, the emphasis in financial reporting was clearly on solvency. Creditors, particularly bankers, were assumed to be the primary users of financial statements. Most bank loans at that time were short term, for what were called self-liquidating purposes. The profitability of a company was not considered relevant in evaluating that type of loan. Creditors, therefore, focused their attention on a company's current financial position as shown on its balance sheet.

Beginning around 1930, accountants began to shift their attention from the needs of short-term creditors to those of long-term equity investors. According to Eldon S. Hendriksen,

> The most important shift in basic accounting thought coming out of the writings and discussions of the late 1920s and early 1930s was the change in the objective of accounting from that of presenting information to management and creditors to that of providing financial information for investors and stockholders.[3]

Along with that change in objective, there was also a shift in emphasis from reporting a company's solvency to reporting its profitability. In 1953 Arthur Stone Dewing commented—

> I have tried to follow, for the last thirty-five years, the changes in the expressed attitude of accountants toward the fundamental tenets of their subject as reflected in the professional journals. The changed attitude toward the income account is one of the most, if not the most, conspicuous development. There has been a steady drift among accountants — especially those who attempt to subject the foundations of their work to critical analysis — toward recognition of the fundamental nature of the income account.[4]

---

3. Eldon S. Hendriksen, *Accounting Theory*, 3d ed. (Homewood, Ill.: Richard D. Irwin, 1977), p.54.
4. Arthur Stone Dewing, *The Financial Policy of Corporations*, 5th ed., 2 vols. (New York: Ronald Press, 1953), 1: 519-520 n.

About that same time, Maurice Moonitz and Charles C. Staehling declared in their accounting textbook that

> The determination of periodical profit or loss from enterprise operations constitutes the crux of the accounting problem, the central issue around which all other considerations revolve and to which they are unavoidably related.[5]

Today, in spite of the great importance of a company's solvency to nearly all financial statement users, the main focus of financial reporting is still on profitability. For many years accounting theorists as well as those groups responsible for promulgating accounting standards have been concerned with income measurement—valuation issues almost exclusively. With few exceptions, reporting information useful in evaluating a company's solvency has either been ignored or given a role clearly secondary to that of reporting profitability information.

Bias toward income measurement and reporting at the expense of solvency reporting shows up in many ways. It sometimes shows up in the way accountants describe business operations and events. The timing of cash receipts and payments is often ignored, and income is referred to as if it were money or cash that can be spent or paid out. Thus, accountants often speak of the retirement of debt and the purchase of plant and equipment "out of profits" when they really mean out of cash generated by operating activities. Also, the income statement is typically referred to as the statement of operations even though it shows only one effect of operations, the income effects of operations—that is, the effects of operations on a company's net assets. Other effects of operations such as those on cash, on liabilities, and on the maturity structure of receivables are not reported in the income statement. In fact, before APB Opinion no. 19 became effective in 1971, CPAs routinely stated in their standard opinion that a company's financial statements "present fairly . . . the results of its operations" even though only the income effects of operations were reported; no statement was required that even purported to report other than the income effects of operations.

Perhaps the strongest evidence of pro-income measurement, anti-solvency bias appears in the accounting profession's response to suggestions by financial statement users that statements of cash receipts and payments would be useful in solvency evaluation because

---

5. Maurice Moonitz and Charles C. Staehling, *Accounting: An Analysis of Its Problems*, 2 vols. (New York: Foundation Press, 1952), 1: 107.

income statements based on accrual accounting conceal the timing of cash movements. Those suggestions have often been interpreted as challenges to the supremacy of the income statement and contemptuously dismissed. For example, in 1961 J.S. Seidman, a prominent practitioner who later became both president of the AICPA and a member of the Accounting Principles Board, stated—

> Instead of studying various ways and terminology for presenting cash flow statements, I think the profession is called upon to report to companies, to analysts, to stockholders, and the exchanges that cash flow figures are dangerous and misleading and the profession will have no part of them.[6]

More recently, statements of cash receipts and payments were rejected by the Financial Accounting Standards Board (FASB) in its exposure draft of *Objectives of Financial Reporting and Elements of Financial Statements of Business Enterprises*. The board explained in paragraphs 33 and 34:

> Financial statements that show only cash receipts and payments during a short period, such as a year, [cannot] adequately indicate whether or not an enterprise's performance is successful.
>
> Information about enterprise earnings (often called net income or net profit) and its components measured by accrual accounting generally provides a better measure of enterprise performance than information about current cash receipts and payments. That is, financial information provided by accounting that recognizes the financial effects of transactions and other events when they occur rather than only when cash is received or paid is usually considered a better basis than cash receipts and payments for estimating an enterprise's present and continuing ability to bring in the cash it needs.[7]

Ruling out statements of cash receipts and payments on the grounds that they cannot "adequately indicate whether or not an enterprise's performance is successful" indicates that the board considered only one aspect of a company's performance to be relevant in measuring success—its earnings performance. Obtaining cash needed to survive and obtaining increased wealth are both necessary parts of an enterprise's performance, or, as Paul Rosenfield put it,

---

6. J. S. Seidman, *Journal of Accountancy*, 111 (June, 1961): 31.
7. FASB, *Objectives of Financial Reporting and Elements of Financial Statements of Business Enterprises* (Stamford, Conn.: FASB, 1977).

"assuring survival and prospering may require different kinds of achievement, not simply different amounts of achievement."[8]

The board's argument that enterprise earnings measured by accrual accounting are a "better" indicator of an enterprise's ability to bring in the cash it needs than information about current cash receipts and payments casts income statements and statements of cash receipts and payments as competing methods of disclosure when they are not. Income statements report the effects of a company's operations on its long-run cash generation; the question when cash has been or will be received or paid is ignored, except as it affects amounts at which receivables and payables are recorded. On the other hand, statements of cash receipts and payments report the effects of operations on cash movements during the year; whether those movements have affected or will affect income is ignored. Thus, income statements and statements of cash receipts and payments are complementary, not competing, forms of disclosure. They report different things for different purposes. The board's rejection of statements of cash receipts and payments at the objectives level, based on the argument that income statements are "better" indicators of an enterprise's ability to generate cash than cash flow statements, indicates an insensitivity to the timing of cash movements and, therefore, an insensitivity to solvency issues.

Scope and Objectives of This Study

This is a study of financial reporting and the evaluation of solvency. It is concerned with the types of information useful to investors, creditors, and other external users of general purpose financial statements in evaluating the present and future solvency of business enterprises.

This study has three objectives. The first and most important is to increase the awareness of accountants in general, and those responsible for setting accounting standards in particular, of the solvency dimension of financial reporting. The second objective is to recommend a decision model that identified the variables relevant in evaluating a company's solvency. The third is to recommend specific changes in financial reporting practices that would increase the usefulness of financial statements in evaluating a company's solvency.

In current practice, a company reports solvency-related information in its financial statements in two principal ways: (a) by classifying

---

8. Paul Rosenfield, "Current Replacement Value Accounting—A Dead End," *Journal of Accountancy*, September, 1975, p. 72.

assets and liabilities as current and noncurrent in its balance sheet and (b) by presenting a statement of changes in financial position as one of the basic financial statements. Both of those practices are examined in detail and evaluated critically in this study. Alternative types of information that would be more useful in evaluating solvency and less confusing to financial statement users are then recommended.

Sources of Information

Three types of information were used in preparing this study: (1) published sources including books, periodicals, pronouncements of authoritative accounting bodies, and corporate annual reports; (2) information on reporting practices obtained from discussion with CPAs and from the files of two large public accounting firms; and (3) interviews and discussions with over fifty CPAs, academic colleagues, and financial statement users including creditors, security analysts, lawyers, and investment bankers selected for their knowledge and understanding of the subject.

Recommendations

The most important recommendation of this study is that accounting policymakers responsible for promulgating accounting standards should give increased attention to the solvency dimension of financial reporting along with the profitability dimension when considering all issues in financial reporting. Specific steps that should now be taken to provide information needed for solvency evaluation include—

1. The current practice of identifying assets and liabilities as current or noncurrent should be discontinued. That practice is based on outmoded concepts of the needs of financial statement users. Continuing that practice in today's environment results in misleading and confusing financial statement users.

2. Liabilities should be classified on the basis of the sources of credit from which they arise as (a) operating liabilities, (b) tax liabilities, and (c) financing liabilities.

3. A schedule of receivables and payables showing the gross amounts and the timing of expected future cash receipts and payments associated with those items should be included as supplementary balance sheet information.

4. Statements of changes in financial position as now prepared should be discontinued and replaced with three required statements: a statement of cash receipts and payments, a statement of financing activities, and a statement of investing activities.

5. The statement of cash receipts and payments should show all sources of cash and all uses of cash and should be accompanied by a separate schedule that shows details of cash received from operations using the direct rather than the "add-back" method (in which depreciation and other noncash expenses are added back to income) of presentation.

6. The statement of financing activities should show all changes in the capital structure of a company regardless of whether those changes affected its cash position. The statement should be divided into two major parts, one that shows debt financing activities and the other that shows equity financing activities.

7. The statement of investing activities should disclose all increases and decreases in long-term investments (including land, plant and equipment, nonmarketable securities, controlled companies, and intangible assets).

2

The Evaluation of Solvency

Financial statement users' needs for information useful in evaluating the solvency of business enterprises have changed greatly during the past several decades. Financial reporting to facilitate that evaluation, however, has changed very little. In other words, financial reporting has not kept pace with the changing information needs of investors, creditors, and other financial statement users concerned with solvency.

The purpose of this chapter is to point out how the evaluation of solvency, or credit analysis as it is usually called, has changed and to provide a decision model of solvency evaluation based on current views of financial writers and analysts. That model is used in later chapters to evaluate current reporting practices for the evaluation of solvency and to suggest alternative methods of reporting.

Early Credit Analysis

According to Arthur Stone Dewing,

> Through long years of banking experience there had grown up a tradition, extending back to the Scotch bankers of the seventeenth century, that the near maturing debts of any corporate enterprise should not exceed a definite ratio to the current capital. The obligations to bankers and merchandise creditors should bear such a relation to the properties of the corporation which are readily convertible into money that no

untoward circumstance would prevent the corporation from having actual money available when each obligation became due.[1]

For many years the core of credit analysis consisted of the analysis of current working capital position, first through the current ratio alone and later through the current ratio combined with other static ratios based on current assets and liabilities, such as the quick or "acid test" ratio and the ratio of working capital to total assets. The following comments are typical of those found in the literature of the 1920s, 1930s, and 1940s.

> Working capital . . . is the measure of a concern's financial solvency. . . .
> The current ratio is the most widely employed of all the . . . ratios, and until recent years was practically the only . . . ratio used in statement analysis work.
> The prominence given to the current ratio as a test for credit is undoubtedly justified.
> Whenever the current ratio, the acid test, and the ratio of current assets to total liabilities are all found to be highly satisfactory, further analysis of . . . ratios may be abandoned as unnecessary.[2]

Although creditors undoubtedly relied on the ability of a debtor to repay its debts out of cash provided by normal operations without having to resort to liquidation, credit analysis centered on the ability of a company to repay its debts if liquidation were to occur, or on what was graphically called its "pounce" value. A. C. Littleton commented:

> So strong was the protection-by-liquidation point of view ("What would the assets bring if sold?") that a balance sheet, even though it was not stated in terms of probable liquidating values, came to rank ahead of a series of income statements as evidence for judging the risk of lending.[3]

---

1. Arthur Stone Dewing, *The Financial Policy of Corporations*, 5th ed., 2 vols. (New York: Ronald Press, 1953), 1: 703 (footnotes omitted).
2. Glenn G. Munn, *Bank Credit: Principles and Operating Procedures* (New York: McGraw-Hill, 1925), pp. 109, 116, 127-129. For similar comments, see Stanley F. Brewster, *Analyzing Credit Risks* (New York: Ronald Press, 1924), pp. 161-162; Mahlon D. Miller, *Bank Loans on Statement and Character* (New York: Ronald Press, 1927), pp. 106-122, 257; and John H. Prime, "Financial Statements and Corporate Reports," chapter 3 of *Fundamentals of Investment Banking*, sponsored by Investment Bankers Association of America (New York: Prentice-Hall, 1949), p. 99.
3. A. C. Littleton, *Structure of Accounting Theory*, American Accounting Association Monograph no. 5 (Urbana, Ill.: American Accounting Asso-

A 1924 textbook explained how the "credit man" of that day should evaluate a credit applicant's risk:

> It is necessary for the credit man to "shade the assets," or to write off a certain percentage merely as a precautionary measure. The important factor is not the applicant's opinion as to the value of his assets, which the listed valuation altogether too frequently represents, but the actual value that will ultimately be realized from them.[4]

It is not surprising that analysis of working capital played so important a role in credit analysis at that time. Fixed assets were considered to have little value in a forced liquidation. Typical bank borrowers often had no long-term liabilities because long-term credit was unavailable to them. Term loans from banks, long-term leasing, and long-term installment sales were not in widespread use until after World War II. Thus, current liabilities were often the only liabilities, and the proceeds from sale of the company's assets were considered the means by which those liabilities would be paid if the debtor were forced to liquidate. The excess of current assets over current liabilities was considered a "cushion" or "margin" or "buffer" that provided security for the payment of those liabilities even if the liquidating value of current assets should turn out to be considerably less than their carrying value. Credit analysis was, therefore, primarily concerned with whether the working capital cushion was "adequate." Roy A. Foulke explained the rationale for the two-to-one current ratio "standard" for measuring working capital adequacy as follows:

> In case of bankruptcy, falling prices, or inflated figures, the book value of current assets could shrink 50 percent in liquidation and current creditors, provided there were no long term creditors, would still receive payment of their obligations in full. For many years, this "two for one" current ratio was the alpha and omega of balance sheet analysis.[5]

---

ciation, 1953), p. 92. Arthur Stone Dewing observed that "bankers have been proverbially interested in statements of . . . net worth of business at liquidation—as if the fundamental value of a working horse were its value for fertilizer" (Dewing, *Financial Policy of Corporations*, 2: 521n).
4. Brewster, *Analyzing Credit Risks*, p. 41.
5. Roy A. Foulke, *Practical Financial Statement Analysis*, 6th ed. (New York: McGraw-Hill, 1968), p. 178. See also A. C. Littleton and V. K. Zimmerman, *Accounting Theory: Continuity and Change* (Englewood Cliffs, N.J.: Prentice-Hall, 1962), p. 116.

Even when viewing the enterprise as a going concern, current working capital position was considered, if not the "alpha and omega," at least the appropriate center for the analyst's attention. Current liabilities were considered obligations that would have to be paid from current assets in the following year. Following that rationale, current assets should "obviously" exceed current liabilities by a reasonable margin so that even if substantial shrinkage should occur in the value of current assets, an enterprise would not have to be liquidated. Harry G. Guthmann, author of several of the most widely used finance textbooks in the 1940s, 1950s, and 1960s explained it as follows:

> No creditor wishes to invite the risks attendant upon liquidation and so the working capital is of vital interest to him, particularly if he is within the class of current liability creditors.
> Current creditors expect payment from current assets, and consequently if the balance sheet is being examined by a banker, a merchant creditor, or any other grantor of short term credit, this portion of the statement will be the center of attention.[6]

William J. Vatter held similar views:

> It is only current assets that represent realizable values that can be depended upon to liquidate claims through the realization of cash; . . . fixed assets are valuable only in the indirect sense, that is, their financial significance arises from their use for specific purposes, . . . More important, . . . to dispose of fixed assets of almost any business would mean cessation of operations.[7]

Widespread criticism of the blind application of the two-to-one current ratio standard appeared during the three decades from 1920 to 1950. Many critics contended that creditors often applied the standard without taking into account the different working capital needs of companies in different industries. Writers concerned themselves with how to take those differences into account to determine whether a company's working capital was adequate and how to supplement the current ratio with other ratios that would help determine either the

---

6. Harry G. Guthmann, *Analysis of Financial Statements*, 4th ed. (New York: Prentice-Hall, 1953), p. 64. See also Jules I. Bogen, *Financial Handbook*, 3d ed. (New York: Ronald Press, 1948), p. 242.
7. William J. Vatter, *The Fund Theory of Accounting and Its Implications for Financial Reports* (Chicago: University of Chicago Press, 1947), p. 64. See also Dewing, *Financial Policy*, 2: 1031n.

adequacy or the quality of working capital, but no real challenge to the supremacy of current working capital position in credit analysis surfaced until the 1950s.

Changing Emphasis in Credit Analysis

The stock market crash of 1929, the depression of the 1930s, and the rapid expansion of nearly all types of business in the late 1940s brought about a searching reappraisal of business practices of all types. Creditors found they were not immune to losses even though they had lent only to companies with "adequate" working capital and they therefore began to question whether working capital was the appropriate basis for the extension of credit. In 1953 Arthur Stone Dewing explained the change in thinking that had occurred as follows:

> Bankers learned by tragic experience that there was no mystical significance in the two-to-one ratio. They observed that in many types of business, under the stress of general disaster, inventories could not be sold, and if such an attempt should be made not a two-to-one or even a three- or four-to-one ratio would bring them the immediate payment of their debts. If the business failed, the relative amounts of current capital in the days before the failure had little significance in the final liquidation of the bankrupt business.[8]

Dewing believed the principal lesson learned from those experiences was that earning power, not current capital, is the "fundamental basis of credit." He concluded—

> The banker has come to understand that the basis of credit is the presumption that the earning power will continue; it is not based on the amount of current capital nor on its selling price, nor on the liquidity of any kind of capital simply as such. Ultimately, he has come to recognize that such a loan can be paid, except through other borrowings, only over the comparatively long period during which the earnings can accumulate. Whatever may have been the tradition of banking, the basis of value, upon which the credit of the corporation must ultimately rest, is the earning power.[9]

Howard and Upton, like Dewing, criticized reliance on current working capital position as the basis for the extension of credit. They

---

8. Dewing, *Financial Policy*, vol. 1, pp. 708-709.
9. Dewing, *Financial Policy*, vol. 1, p. 710.

believed, however, that the proper basis is the ability of a company to generate cash in the relatively near future, not its earning power. They argued—

> It should be clear that the real problem in judging a business's short term financial position is to ascertain as closely as possible the future cash generating ability of the business in relation to the claims upon cash that will have to be met within the near future. . . . It matters not what conditions prevail at a given time; the important thing is whether the business in performing its regular operating functions can continue to generate cash in sufficient quantity and in satisfactory time to meet all operating and financial obligations.[10]

A few years later James E. Walter explained further the role of static working capital analysis in evaluating a company's ability to pay its debts. After describing static working capital analysis as a form of "partial analysis" that "encourages the neglect of certain other highly relevant matters" he attempted to develop an integrated structure of analysis that takes into account future cash flows. He explained it as follows:

> In the development of an integrated structure at least three points merit consideration. One is that the true source of funds which underlies net cash flows is sales. A second is that current liabilities (as of January 1) do not represent the sum total of cash outlays anticipated within the forthcoming period. The third point is that acceptance of the going concern hypothesis implies that neither current assets nor current liabilities are reducible to zero. . . .
> Current liabilities are never wholly discharged; nor—by analogous reasoning—are current assets ever entirely available to meet currently maturing obligations.[11]

Current Views of Credit Analysis

Cash Flows. The views expressed by Howard and Upton and by Walter in the 1950s are widely accepted by financial analysts today. In recent years, emphasis in solvency analysis has shifted from static analysis of current working capital position to dynamic analysis of future cash flows in much the same way that the emphasis in security

---

10. Bion B. Howard and Miller Upton, *Introduction to Business Finance* (New York: McGraw-Hill, 1953), p. 135.
11. James E. Walter, "Determination of Technical Solvency," *Journal of Business*, 30, no. 1 (January, 1957): 32, 38, and 43.

analysis shifted from static analysis of balance sheet values to dynamic analysis of capitalized net income some thirty or forty years earlier.[12]

The central question in solvency analysis today is whether the cash expected to be received within a given time period will equal or exceed required cash payments within that same period. A balance sheet does not provide that information. A company's principal sources of cash are from sale of its products or services to its customers and from borrowing and issuance of stock to investors. Its principal uses include payments to employees, suppliers, and government, repayment of debt, and purchase of plant and equipment. Most of the cash a company will receive within the following year is not represented by balance sheet assets now on hand and most of the obligations that will have to be met are not shown as liabilities.

The old concept of current assets as the source from which current liabilities will be paid is meaningless under this framework of analysis (if it ever had any meaning). Current liabilities are not paid with current assets; they are paid with cash. Whether a firm's current or its noncurrent assets were the source of its cash is an unanswerable question. One can no more determine whether current or noncurrent assets provided the cash generated by operations than he can determine which blade of the scissors cut the cloth, for both were clearly necessary.[13]

Confusion still surrounds the distinction between the earning power and the short-run cash generating ability of a firm but considerable progress has been made in clarifying that relationship in recent years.[14] The financial failures of the late 1960s and early 1970s drove home the point that debts are not paid out of profits in much the same unforgiving way that the failures of the 1930s drove home the point that current liabilities are not paid out of current assets. To use an

---

12. For a discussion of this shift in security analysis, see Benjamin Graham, David L. Dodd, and Sidney Cottle, *Security Analysis: Principles and Technique*, 4th ed. (New York: McGraw-Hill, 1962), p. 214.
13. Raymond J. Chambers observed that "there is . . . no foundation in business or economic reasoning for drawing a distinction between 'fixed assets' and current assets on the ground that the former are 'not held for sale or conversion into cash.' It is incontrovertible that nonmonetary assets are acquired and held only so that they may be converted into cash through the sale of the product of their services, and, or, their resale" (*Accounting, Evaluation and Economic Behavior* (Englewood Cliffs, N.J.: Prentice-Hall, 1966), p. 198).
14. See further discussion of this point in chapter 6.

expression of the courts, profits are a "quantum and not a res"—they are an intangible measure and not a physical thing. They are a *change* in wealth measured in monetary units but they are not money.

Profits are measured by the excess of revenue over the related expenses of a firm during a given period of time. A dollar either has been or is expected to be received at some time during the life of the enterprise for each dollar of revenue recognized during a given period, and a dollar either has been or is expected to be paid out at some time for each dollar of expense matched with that revenue.[15] However, because of the leads and lags between revenue recognition and cash receipts and because of the leads and lags between cash payments and expense recognition, the amount of cash generated by a company during a short period of time such as a year will equal its reported profit for that period only by chance. While profits measured in units of money (not units of general purchasing power) for the entire lifetime of a firm must equal its net cash flow from operations for that period, a profitable firm may experience substantial net cash outflows over extended periods of time. The creditor who ignores or confuses the distinction between earning power and short-run cash generating ability is likely to pay dearly for his mistakes. Sophisticated creditors today focus their attention on a firm's future cash flows because they know that even a high level of profits does not guarantee that sufficient cash will be on hand to pay debts when they fall due. Many use complex financial models to determine the effect of various assumed levels of sales and profits on future cash receipts and payments.

Undoubtedly one of the reasons for the heavy reliance on static working capital position in early credit analysis was that balance sheets were typically the only financial statements available to creditors. Early textbooks in credit analysis refer to a company's balance sheet as "*the* financial statement."[16] Although income statements were typically provided as early as the 1930s, the presentation of funds statements or statements of changes in financial position was not even recommended by the AICPA until 1963 and was not required until 1971. It is not clear which was the primary cause, whether increased understanding of the dynamic nature of

---

15. For discussion of this point, see Reed K. Storey, "Cash Movements and Periodic Income Determination," *Accounting Review*, 36 (July, 1960): 449-454.
16. See, for example, Munn, *Bank Credit*, p. 84 and Miller, *Bank Loans*, p. 78.

fund flows led to increased use of funds statements or whether increased availability of funds statements led to increased understanding of fund flows. The two were probably self-reinforcing, but the important point is that the increased availability of funds statements has undoubtedly led to decreased emphasis on current working capital position in credit analysis in much the same way that increased availability of income statements led to a decreased emphasis on balance sheet values in security analysis.

Financial Position. To say that creditors and other financial statement users concerned with solvency now focus their primary attention on whether a company's cash receipts will be adequate to cover its required cash payments does not, of course, mean that they are no longer concerned with a company's financial position. They clearly are, but not for the same reason they once were. The focus of their concern is now quite different.

One obvious reason for a creditor's interest in the financial position of a company is that a statement of financial position may provide some of the information needed to estimate future cash receipts and payments. The amounts and due dates of receivables and payables are obvious examples, but there are also many less obvious examples such as the age of plant and equipment, the replacement cost of plant and equipment, and the amount of unused tax loss carryforwards.

There is, however, a second reason for a creditor's interest in financial position, which may be even more important than the one just mentioned. It stems from the nature of forecasts. A forecast of cash receipts and payments is based on assumptions about what will happen in the future; inevitably, some assumptions turn out to be wrong. Creditors are vitally interested in what is likely to happen to a company if events do *not* turn out as expected. This does not mean, however, that they adopt a liquidating or pounce value approach. A creditor forces a company into liquidation only as a last resort,[17] and, therefore, a debtor's ability to control its cash receipts and payments and thereby adapt or adjust to unexpected events is of greater

---

17. Dewing noted that "Liquidation under bankruptcy is very costly, very tedious, and invariably disappointing. . . . In the end, after the court, the trustee in bankruptcy, and the preferred claimants are paid, very little remains for the general creditors—and the banks and merchandise creditors will get only a small proportion of this very little" (Dewing, *Financial Policy*, 1: 709n).

concern to a creditor than the pounce value of a debtor's assets. This capacity to control cash receipts and payments to survive a period of financial adversity may be referred to as a company's financial flexibility.[18] Financial flexibility depends in part on a company's financial position. The nature of financial flexibility and the types of information useful in evaluating it are discussed in the next section.

Financial Flexibility

A *financially flexible company* may be defined as one that can take corrective action that will eliminate an excess of required cash payments over expected cash receipts quickly and with minor adverse effect on present or future earnings or on the market value of its stock.

To illustrate the nature of financial flexibility, assume a company's expected cash receipts are adequate to cover its required cash payments. Several things may occur that would tend to disturb this equilibrium and, if corrective action is not taken, lead to insolvency. First, cash receipts may be less than anticipated due to a decline in sales, a slowdown in collection of receivables, a decline in dividends from investee companies, an unwillingness by lenders to extend credit to the limit contemplated in the financial plan, and so forth. Second, cash payments to suppliers of goods and services may increase because of price or wage increases, increased consumption of goods and services, and so forth. How much a given decline in sales will affect a company's net cash flow depends on the responsiveness of cash payments to changes in sales. If a large proportion of operating cash payments vary directly with sales volume, a given decline in sales will not, of course, affect net cash flow from operations as much as if the operating cash payments are unresponsive to sales declines. Third, a company may experience extraordinary or unusual cash payments due to uninsured catastrophic losses, assessment of additional taxes for prior years, and so forth. When cash flows do not occur as planned or predicted by financial management and a cash drain is likely, a company's ability to avoid insolvency depends on its financial flexibility.

The principal strategies that companies use to take corrective action to avoid insolvency include—

---

18. The concept of financial flexibility is similar to the concept of financial mobility in Gordon Donaldson, *Strategy for Financial Mobility* (Boston: Harvard University Press, 1969). That book is the source of many of the ideas in this section.

1. Borrowing money.

   a. Directly, by borrowing from banks, selling bonds, selling commercial paper, and so forth.

   b. Indirectly, by delaying payments to trade creditors, extending due dates of loans, and so forth.

2. Liquidating assets.

   a. Directly, by selling marketable securities, factoring receivables, selling (possibly combined with leaseback) plant and equipment, and so forth.

   b. Indirectly, by failing to replace inventory as it is sold through normal trade channels, failing to replace fixed assets as they are consumed in operations, and so forth.

3. Reducing costs.

4. Reducing dividends.

5. Issuing capital stock.

The variables that determine a company's financial flexibility are discussed below.

Borrowing Capacity. A company's capacity to borrow in time of need depends on many things. Its relations with creditors, its prearranged lines of credit and credit commitments, the amount of its present debt, its record of earnings, and its record of debt repayment all influence its present capacity to borrow.

Asset Disposability. The ability of a company to raise cash by liquidating some of its assets in time of need depends primarily on two basic attributes of those assets: their interdependence in use and their price characteristics.

Some companies can dispose of a portion of their assets without significantly impairing the profitability of those remaining because their assets are not interdependent in the production of earnings. A company holding only marketable securites, for example, could dispose of some of them without significantly impairing the profitability of its other securities. Other companies, however, hold assets that are so interdependent in the way they are used that disposal of some of them reduces significantly or destroys the profitability of those remaining. For example, a railroad company with one train and a single line of track between two major terminals could not dispose of either asset without significantly impairing the profitability of the other.

The interdependence of a company's assets depends on the quantities held of a given type of asset as well as the way they are used. A company with inventories in excess of normal needs, for example, could readily dispose of some of them without significantly impairing the profitability of its other assets, but as inventories reach some minimum level, further reduction would tend to destroy the profitability of other assets.

A company's ability to dispose of a portion of its assets without adversely affecting its present or future earnings also depends on the price characteristics of its assets.

One such characteristic is marketability. The marketability of an asset refers to the spread at any time between the purchase price of that asset and the price at which it could be sold in forced liquidation. Assets with narrow price spreads are relatively marketable. Marketability of its assets tends to increase a company's financial flexibility.

Price volatility of a company's assets also affects its financial flexibility. If the book value of an asset exceeds its market value, management may avoid liquidating it to relieve a temporary cash shortage because of the loss that would have to be reported. Assets with stable market prices tend to increase the financial flexibility of a company.

Historically, only assets classified as current have been considered available for liquidation in time of financial adversity. According to conventional wisdom, a firm in financial difficulty can contract the size of its current assets, particularly its inventory, but it cannot dispose of its fixed assets and still remain a going concern. That has always been an oversimplification (there is obviously some minimum amount of inventory a company must have to operate), but it is even more of an oversimplification today than it used to be because of new business practices and new methods of financing.

Firms in financial difficulty today increasingly look to their fixed rather that their current assets for solutions to their problems. Fixed assets are viewed as much less permanent than they once were. In an interview, one businessman said: "Everything in this company is for sale if the price is right. If you offer me enough for the desk I am writing on I'll clean it out immediately." Today a conglomerate may sell a complete division or segment of its operations, a retail chain may close some of its outlets and liquidate the stores and land if it owns them, and a manufacturer may sell and lease back some of its plant and equipment to raise cash. Or, even if it is unable to sell its present equipment, it may replace it with leased equipment as it wears out and thereby increase its net cash flow over what it would have been had it purchased new equipment.

Cost Flexibility. The cost flexibility of a company refers to the extent to which costs can be reduced during a period of financial difficulty without impairing long-run profitability. A company that can postpone maintenance or research and development without incurring greatly increased total costs or decreased revenues over a longer period of time, as a consequence, tends to have greater financial flexibility than a company that cannot postpone expenditures without seriously impairing its long-run profitability.

Dividend Flexibility. Reduction of dividends may also be used to cope with financial difficulty, but the ability of companies to do this varies greatly. Dividend flexibility refers to the ability of a company to reduce its dividends during a cash shortage. A company that is not currently paying any dividends obviously has no dividend flexibility. A company with a history of stable or steadily increasing dividends to which it has pointed with pride has less dividend flexibility than a company that pays a small amount of regular dividends and describes the major portion of its payments as "extras" that vary from year to year. Dividend flexibility increases a company's financial flexibility.

Stock Flexibility. Almost all companies can raise cash by issuing additional stock, but their ability to do so on favorable terms whenever they wish varies greatly. A company whose stock is widely held, that operates in a stable industry, and that has a long history of stable or steadily increasing earnings and dividends is more likely to be able to issue stock on favorable terms whenever it wishes than a closely held company in a volatile industry. The ability to issue stock at any time without depressing the market excessively may be referred to as stock flexibility. Stock flexibility tends to increase financial flexibility.

Conclusion

The decision model described in this chapter identifies the future cash receipts and payments of a business enterprise as the primary concern of analysts when evaluating solvency and financial flexibility as the secondary concern. That model is based on discussions in the literature of finance and discussions with practicing financial analysts.

Since financial analysis is an art rather than a science there is far from perfect agreement on exactly how to go about deciding whether to grant credit to or invest in a particular company, but there is substantial agreement on the relevance of the variables identified in the above discussion and the rationale underlying those variables. The real differences are found in exactly how to estimate future cash receipts and payments and how to take into account some of the attributes that make up the financial flexibility of a company.

Financial ratios are widely used by practicing financial analysts. Ratio analysis, however, is not an alternative to solvency analysis based on expected future cash receipts and payments and on financial flexibility. Ratios are simply tools; they are merely a way of comparing one variable with another. Some ratios are used to evaluate various aspects of a company's financial flexibility. The debt-equity ratio, for example, is likely to provide some insight into a company's unused borrowing capacity, and asset turnover ratios are likely to provide insight into asset disposability. Empirical evidence of the power of financial ratios to predict financial failure is examined in chapter 4.

3

Historical Development of Balance Sheet Classification Practice

After describing a 1571 balance sheet that "shows a clear conception of the difference between current capital and fixed capital," Arthur Stone Dewing observes that "it is of significance that after over three and a half centuries of English accounting this distinction has remained of essential and fundamental importance."[1] A practice based on such a time-honored distinction should not be discarded lightly. A strong case needs to be made for why change is now necessary. The principal argument used in this study for discontinuing present practice is that it does not meet the current needs of financial statement users. This chapter explains why practice developed the way it did. It traces the evolution of current practice and examines the underlying forces that gave rise to that practice in an effort to provide background for the specific arguments presented in chapter 4 for discontinuing that practice.

---

1. Arthur Stone Dewing, *Financial Policy of Corporations*, 5th ed., 2 vols. (New York: Ronald Press, 1951), 1: 685n.

Origin and Influence of Asset Classification Concepts

Origin in Economics. The first extended discussion of the distinction between current or circulating capital and fixed capital is found in the writings of the classical economists during the 18th and 19th centuries. Adam Smith, for example, observed:

> There are two different ways in which a capital may be employed so as to yield a revenue or profit to its employer.
>
> First, it may be employed in raising, manufacturing or purchasing goods, and selling them again with a profit. The capital employed in this manner yields no revenue or profits to its employer, while it remains in his possession, or continues in the same shape. The goods of the merchant yield him no revenue or profit till he sells them for money, and the money yields him as little till it is again exchanged for goods. His capital is continually going from him in one shape, and returning to him in another, and it is only by means of such circulation, or successive exchanges, that it can yield him any profit. Such capitals, therefore, may very properly be called circulating capitals.
>
> Secondly, it may be employed in the improvements of land, in the purchase of useful machines and instruments of trade or in such-like things as yield a revenue or profit without changing master, or circulating any further. Such capitals, therefore, may very properly be called fixed capitals.[2]

David Ricardo considered circulating capital to be capital used in the "support of labour" as opposed to "capital of a comparatively fixed and durable character" such as "implements, machines and buildings" which he believed were used as a substitute for labor rather than to support it.[3] John Stuart Mill also distinguished between fixed and circulating capital, but to him the distinction rested on whether the capital "fulfills the whole of its office . . . by a single use" (circulating capital) or whether "its efficacy . . . is prolonged through many repetitions of the productive operation" (fixed capital).[4]

Double-Account Balance Sheet. The double-account balance sheet, a form of financial statement prescribed for railroads and other public works in England during the 19th century, was based on the

---

2. Adam Smith, *The Wealth of Nations* (New York: Random House, 1937), pp. 262-263.
3. David Ricardo, *The Principles of Political Economy and Taxation* (New York: E.P. Dutton & Co., 1917), p. 53.
4. John Stuart Mill, *Principles of Political Economy*, rev. ed. (New York: Colonial Press, 1899), p. 57.

distinction between fixed and circulating capital. The term "double-account" referred to a form of balance sheet in which fixed assets, long-term debt, and owners' equity were reported in one section and circulating assets and short-term debt were reported in another. The excess of the sum of long-term debt and owners' equity over fixed assets was reported as a debit in the long-term section and a credit in the short-term section.

The double-account balance sheet was first prescribed for British Parliamentary Companies organized to undertake "permanent" public works such as canals, railroads, and similar projects but it was never widely used, even in England. It has, however, been referred to frequently in accounting literature and many prominent writers have advocated its use as a means of highlighting or emphasizing the distinction between fixed and circulating capital.[5] According to William J. Vatter, the report form of balance sheet sometimes used today is an outgrowth of the double-account balance sheet.[6]

Early Court Decisions. The distinction between fixed and circulating capital was the basis of the court's decision in several important British cases dealing with the measurement of income for the purpose of determining whether dividends had been legally declared. The first of those cases was brought by a common shareholder in 1889 to restrain the payment of dividends on preferred stock on the grounds that income was inadequate to cover the proposed dividends (*Lee v. Neuchtal Asphalt Company*, 41 C.D. 13 (1889)). The specific point in controversy was whether amortization of the cost of certain long-term leases on mining property should be deducted in calculating net income available for dividends. The court held that it need not be and justified its decision by reference to "the distinction drawn by economists, which is a very substantial one, between fixed capital, the money expended in purchasing which is sunk once and for all, and circulating capital, like stock-in-trade which in the ordinary course of business, is parted with and replaced by other."

Several years later, the same judge elaborated his views in another dividend case, *Verner v. General and Commercial Investment*

---

5. For discussion and citations see William J. Vatter, *The Fund Theory of Accounting and Its Implications for Financial Reports* (Chicago: University of Chicago Press, 1947), pp. 60-64 and "A Direct Method for the Preparation of Fund Statements," *Journal of Accountancy*, 77 (April, 1944): 479n.
6. Vatter, *Fund Theory of Accounting*, p. 64.

Trust (2 Ch. 239 (1894)). In that case the defendant's operating revenue from dividends and interest exceeded current operating expenses, but the value of its fixed assets had declined nearly 50 percent. The court held as follows:

> fixed capital may be sunk and lost, and yet the excess of current receipts over current expenses may be applied in payment of a dividend, though where the income of a Company arises from the turning over of circulating capital no dividend can be paid unless the circulating capital is kept up to its original value, as otherwise there would be a payment of dividend out of capital.

Asset Valuation Practices. The *Neuchtal* and *Verner* cases did not result in balance sheet identification of fixed and circulating capital, but they influenced the development of valuation rules that are still followed both in England and in the United States. Shortly after those cases were decided, Dicksee reasoned that "the values of all 'floating assets' should be stated in Balance Sheets on the basis of what they are actually worth to a going concern at the time of balancing," but "it is incorrect to take into account fluctuations in the value of what his lordship called 'capital assets,' but what we (as accountants) would call 'fixed assets'."[7]

A few years later Dicksee explained this in greater detail:

> The justification for thus ignoring fluctuations in the value of capital assets is that these assets have been acquired, and are being permanently retained, not with a view to their being eventually realized at a profit in the ordinary course of business, but with a view to their being *used* for the purpose of enabling trading profits to be made in other ways. . . .
> In the case, however, of assets which it is not intended to retain and utilize in the business (as for example, Stock, Bank Debts, or temporary investments), a wholly different question arises. Here, if the accounts are to be upon a sound basis, it is important not to lose sight of the fact that the whole object of the business is to convert these items into cash at the earliest possible moment, or at any moment which may be thought convenient. In every case therefore the intrinsic value at the moment is clearly a potent factor, and any shrinkage that may have taken place must consequently be regarded as a realized loss, if the accounts are kept upon a sound basis, and as such it must be deducted

---

7. Lawrence R. Dicksee, "Goodwill and Its Treatment in Accounts," *Accountant* (England), 23 (January 9, 1897): 45.

from the value of the asset and debited to Revenue. *Per Contra* appreciations in the value of the floating assets might with equal propriety be credited to Revenue but as, pending actual realization, there must always be a doubt as to whether any such appreciation has actually occurred, it is only prudent to postpone taking credit for the assumed profit until such time as it has actually been earned.[8]

In this country, Hatfield attributed the fact that the cost or market rule was applied to circulating but not to fixed assets to the "distinction of great importance" between those two types of assets. He explained,

> There is coming to be recognized a difference in the basis of valuation of these two classes of assets, which permits much greater latitude in regard to fixed assets. In general it is considered legitimate to continue fixed assets at their cost despite a subsequent decline in their value. But in valuing circulating assets regard must be had to current values, although there is some question as to whether the market value, even of circulating assets, can be accepted where that exceeds the original cost.[9]

If different valuation rules were to be used for fixed or "capital" assets than were used for circulating or "floating" assets, accountants obviously needed to know which assets were fixed and which were circulating, and it would seem to be a logical step to identify those different types on a company's balance sheet. Surprisingly, that step was never taken either in England or the United States. Balance sheet grouping or classification of assets did not develop in England until required by the Companies Act of 1947.[10] While it developed much earlier in this country for other reasons to be explained in the following section, early practice was not based on the fixed-circulating dichotomy. The roots of that dichotomy were, however, deeply embedded in accounting thought to be resurrected at a later time.

---

8. Lawrence R. Dicksee, *Advanced Accounting* (London: Gee & Co., 1903), p. 5.
9. Henry Rand Hatfield, *Modern Accounting* (New York: D. Appleton, 1909), p. 81. Also found in Henry Rand Hatfield, *Accounting: Its Principles and Problems* (New York: D. Appleton, 1927), p. 75.
10. William Huizingh, *Working Capital Classification* (Ann Arbor, Mich.: University of Michigan, 1967), p. 52.

Evolution of Classification in American Practice

According to William Huizingh,

> Classification of balance sheet items was rare prior to 1900, either in textbooks of that period or in published statements. Yet the practice of grouping assets according to certain characteristics they shared became almost a universally accepted reporting technique during the first two decades of the present century.[11]

A 1945 survey conducted by Roy A. Foulke[12] confirms that view. He asked twenty-five of the older public accounting firms when they began using the terms "current assets" and "current liabilities" in their practices. Although most of them responded that they had no records that would provide that information, the following six were able to give approximate dates:

Haskins & Sells	1898
Pogson, Peloubet & Co.	1905
Peat, Marwick, Mitchell & Co.	1906
Niles and Niles	1907
Leslie, Banks & Company	1910
F. W. Lafrentz & Co.	before 1914

Bankers' Influence on Early U.S. Practice. The fact that balance sheet classification developed much earlier in the United States than in Great Britain was the result of different influences on accounting and auditing practices in those two countries. Wild speculation in joint stock company shares during the late seventeenth and early eighteenth centuries in Great Britain resulted in the "Bubble Act" of 1719, which prohibited the creation of joint stock companies. Although that legislation was repealed in 1825 and limited liability companies were again permitted, they were required by statute to maintain adequate accounting records and to submit annual audited balance sheets to their shareholders and to the government.[13] According to Huizingh,

---

11. Huizingh, *Working Capital*, p. 46.
12. Roy A. Foulke, *Practical Financial Statement Analysis*, 6th ed. (New York: McGraw-Hill, 1968), p. 189.
13. Huizingh, *Working Capital*, p. 61.

auditing functions and standards in Great Britain were largely formulated in response to statutory requirement. Auditors were regarded as the agents of the stockholders, responsible for submitting to their principals a report of stewardship of the directors' activities. Not surprisingly, balance sheets prepared in the light of this background emphasized the discharge of responsibility by directors, displaying most prominently the measure of accountability (capital) and largely ignoring the question of liquidity as being of no great interest to stockholders.[14]

Early influences on U.S. accounting and auditing were quite different. Most businesses were not required by law to maintain adequate accounting records or to report regularly to stockholders. According to Huizingh, the need for financial statements other than those prepared for management arose primarily from the way in which short-term bank financing developed in the United States:

> In contrast to the practice in Great Britain, where trade acceptances were widely used, there developed in this country soon after the War between the States the practice of purchase on open account. Since bankers were no longer able to obtain two-name discounted commercial paper in the form of acceptances, they found it desirable to offer short-term financing to business ventures in the form of promissory notes. But, having foregone the security of double protection, they sensed the need of obtaining more adequate and more reliable financial information from their clients. Hence, a demand for audited statements arose—and bankers, being the foremost users of such statements, were in a position to influence the standards of form and valuation adopted.[15]

The strong influence of credit grantors, particularly bankers, on the development of accounting in the early decades of this century is widely recognized in accounting literature. Paul-Joseph Esquerre, writing in 1927, observed—

> It is undeniable that today almost every business balance sheet proceeds on the assumption that it is going to be used to obtain bank loans; and as the banker is presumed to loan only on the security of liquid assets, all the efforts of the statement of financial status are directed towards the proof of that liquidity.[16]

---

14. Huizingh, *Working Capital*, p. 61.
15. Huizingh, *Working Capital*, p. 62.
16. Paul-Joseph Esquerre, *Accounting* (New York: Ronald Press, 1927), p. 41.

Hector R. Anton later commented:

> The great historical influence of bankers on financial statements cannot be overemphasized. Preparation of statements for the granting of credit influenced not only the statements themselves but accounting principles as well.[17]

Undoubtedly one of the reasons accountants were so willing to listen to bankers early in the century was that "the insistence of credit men on audited statements contributed mightily to the growth of our profession" at a time when there were few laws requiring the use of public auditors, and credit men, therefore, "were excellent friends of the accounting profession."[18]

As explained in chapter 2, credit analysis during the early part of this century was dominated by the liquidating or pounce value point of view. It is not surprising, therefore, that this point of view, in turn, dominated classification at that time. The emphasis was not on which assets would *normally* be converted into cash within a year but which ones *could* be converted. Thus it was reasoned that the cash surrender value of life insurance, for example, should be included whereas prepaid expenses should be excluded. Huizingh noted that "by 1920 most classification was based on the relative liquidity of the assets, that is, their ability to be converted into cash in the short run to meet maturing obligations."[19]

Conflicting Early Practice. Classification based on liquidity was not developed by an authoritative group and then adopted by all or even a majority of accountants. Classification practice evolved slowly. Several different methods were used in practice both before and after 1920, and many more were advocated in accounting literature.

Many different terms were used to describe asset categories during the early part of the century. Contrary to present practice in

---

17. Hector R. Anton, *Accounting for the Flow of Funds* (New York: Houghton Mifflin, 1962), p. 5. For further discussion of this point, see A. C. Littleton and V. K. Zimmerman, *Accounting Theory: Continuity and Change*, (Englewood Cliffs, N.J.: Prentice-Hall, 1962), pp. 113-117; and Eldon S. Hendriksen, *Accounting Theory*, 3d ed. (Homewood, Ill.: Richard D. Irwin, 1977), pp. 56-59.
18. Stephen Gilman, "Accounting Principles and the Current Classification," *Accounting Review*, 19 (April, 1944): 111.
19. Huizingh, *Working Capital*, p. 60.

which the term "quick" assets usually refers only to cash, receivables, and marketable securites, that term was often used as a synonym for current assets.[20] Sometimes, however, it was applied to a subcategory of current assets, namely cash, trade receivables, and inventory—excluding only marketable securities and receivables from stockholders, officers, and employees.[21] Other terms used to describe what would now be called current assets included circulating, liquid, and floating.

One of the more interesting classifications used early in the century was to identify separately inventories and deferred charges as "working" or "current working" assets. An accountant with many years of experience with one of the older public accounting firms described the evolution of those terms as follows:

> About the turn of the century, we sometimes used the classification of current assets, but with a separate classification of current working assets, the latter including inventories, generally the major items, deferred charges, stores, and the like. In or about 1906 the classification evolved into "current and working assets," the descriptive term for what is now simply "current assets." Two or three years later we find "current assets" and "current liabilities" but "current and working" was still good verbal mintage, and, as I recall it, the subject of intermittent informal discussion. The decline and fall of the description "working assets" either as a separate term, or as a constituent of "current and working" dates, I would say, from 1915 or thereabouts.[22]

Some writers distinguished between fixed, current, and deferred assets. Deferred assets consisted of "certain payments made for the benefit of future periods, or certain fixed charges paid in advance . . . such as taxes, interest, and insurance premiums."[23]

---

20. See, for example, Stanley F. Brewster, *Analyzing Credit Risks* (New York: Ronald Press, 1924), p. 58 and Glenn G. Munn, *Bank Credit: Principles and Operating Procedures* (New York: McGraw-Hill, 1925), p. 108.
21. It was used this way in the balance sheet form recommended by the Federal Reserve Board in 1917. See Federal Reserve Board, *Approved Methods for the Preparation of Balance Sheet Statements*, 1918. This pamphlet was reprinted from the *Federal Reserve Bulletin*, April, 1917, where it appeared under the title "Uniform Accounting."
22. Related to Roy A. Foulke in 1945 and reported by him in his *Practical Financial Statement Analysis*, p. 189.
23. Brewster, *Analyzing Credit Risks*, p. 59. See also Munn, *Bank Credit*, p. 107, and Roy B. Kester, *Accounting Theory and Practice*, 2 vols. (New York: Ronald Press, 1918), 2: 96.

The practice of classifying inventories and deferred charges or prepayments as noncurrent assets or as a separate category within current assets probably resulted from a conflict between the bankers' liquidating point of view and the fixed-circulating distinction developed by the early economists. Inventories and prepayments clearly fit the concept of a circulating asset in the sense that they were held by the firm for relatively short periods of time and were constantly being replaced with other similar assets rather than used for long periods of time to produce goods which would, in turn, be sold. On the other hand, when looked at through the eyes of the banker, those assets were clearly different in some sense from cash and receivables. The liquidating value of inventories was subject to much wider fluctuations than cash or receivables, and the question often arose whether deferred charges would yield anything at all on liquidation.

The conflict between the economist's circulating concept and the banker's liquidating approach can be seen clearly in the writings of William Morse Cole. In 1910 he vacillated between the two approaches. He first stated that a balance sheet

> should be so arranged as to indicate not only what is the ultimate solvency—that is, how much in the course of time may be realized on property as an offset against debt—but also how much of the property can be converted at once into a medium for paying debts.[24]

Three pages later he concluded that supplies should be classified as current assets on the ground that

> The real purpose of the current group of items in the balance sheet is not so much to distinguish what can be immediately converted into cash as to show those items which in the ordinary conduct of the business can be turned over readily for the purposes of the business.[25]

In 1915 he clearly embraced the liquidating point of view when he defined current assets as "all items that can be readily converted into cash."[26]

---

24. William Morse Cole, *Accounting and Auditing* (Chicago: Home Study Publishing Co., 1910), p. 315.
25. Cole, *Accounting and Auditing*, p. 318.
26. William Morse Cole, *Accounts: Their Construction and Interpretation*, rev. and enl. ed. (Boston: Houghton Mifflin, 1915), p. 222.

Controversy in Accounting Literature. Balance sheet classification continued to be a topic of frequent debate in accounting literature throughout the 1920s and 1930s. Two of the principal figures in the controversy were Maurice Peloubet and Anson Herrick. Peloubet charged in 1928 that

> The present method . . . of arranging the various items on a balance-sheet is not clear, logical nor informing. It is a hybrid resulting from the conflict of the desire of the accountant and businessman for a statement on a true going-concern basis and the demand of the banker and possibly some portion of the investing public for a statement which is, to all intents and purposes, on a liquidation basis.[27]

He went on to point out, as many did after him, that if accountants adopt a going concern point of view,

> the raw material required to keep the factory or mill in operation, the supplies required to be kept on hand for operating or emergency purposes, the receivables necessarily carried by reason of credit terms and the cash needed to finance payrolls and purchases are fixed and permanent investment of money in the enterprise to the same extent that land, buildings and machinery are . . . . If the business falls off they may be realized in part but it is equally true that part of the plant may be sold under other conditions also.[28]

Herrick, a practitioner who was later to play an important role as member of the committee on accounting procedure in the development of Accounting Research Bulletin no. 30 on the subject of working capital, first published his views on the subject in the January, 1932, issue of the *Journal of Accountancy*. He first seemed to align himself on the side of the banker with the comment that "the current section of a balance-sheet is of predominant interest and importance to the banker,"[29] but he then went on to define current assets in a way that seems more compatible with the economist's circulating capital concept than the banker's liquidating approach. Dicksee had described fixed assets forty years before as "those *with* which business is

---

27. Maurice E. Peloubet, "Current Assets and the Going Concern," *Journal of Accountancy*, 46 (July, 1928): 19.
28. Peloubet, "Current Assets," p. 20.
29. Anson Herrick, "What Should Be Included in Current Assets?" *Journal of Accountancy*, 53 (January, 1932): 51.

carried on," and circulating assets as "those *in* which business is carried on."[30] Herrick defined current asssets as

> those assets employed in and comprising a necessary part of the trading or operating cycle of an enterprise, as opposed to those assets *with which* an enterprise operates. . . . current assets embrace all property concerned with and at any point in the cycle which will, within the period of the cycle, become transformed into money.[31]

He criticized the then popular practice of classifying cash surrender value of life insurance as a current asset on the grounds that it was "in opposition to correct business, as well as accounting principles."[32]

A few months later, Peloubet attacked Herricks's views in a letter to the *Journal of Accountancy*:

> It was somewhat disappointing to read in the January 1932 number of *The Journal* an article by Anson Herrick in which he seems to arrange himself on the side of the banker by agreeing to the anomalous distinction between fixed and current assets, while suggesting a few revisions of the theory as to what is usually included in current assets. It is surely time for us to attempt to break away from the impossible and illogical situation into which we are forced by applying liquidation principles to going concerns and to come out boldly and say that assets are either invested in the business or are unnecessary to the conduct of the business. Merely to say that they might be turned into cash without stating whether that cash must be immediately reinvested or may be disbursed to stockholders is an evasion of an issue which present conditions emphasize.[33]

Waning Influence of Bankers. During the 1930s and early 1940s there seemed to be growing agreement among accountants that the banker's pounce value concept was not appropriate as a criterion for distinguishing between current and noncurrent assets and a different approach was needed. The reason for this is not entirely clear. Accountants argued that pounce value conflicts with the going concern concept, but the vehemence of some of the articles written at the time

---

30. Lawrence R. Dicksee, *Auditing*, ed. Robert H. Montgomery, American ed. rev. (New York: Ronald Press, 1909), p. 183 (emphasis original).
31. Herrick, "What Should Be Included in Current Assets?" p. 51, (emphasis original).
32. Herrick, "What Should Be Included in Current Assets?" p. 58.
33. Maurice E. Peloubet, letter to the editor, *Journal of Accountancy*, 53 (April, 1932): 310.

suggests that a more important reason may have been resentment by some accountants at what might be called "banker's influence." Gilman, for example, described a "good banker" as a

> pessimist who dislikes to admit, even to himself, that a customer's debts will be paid as the normal result of operations and who expects to impound cash from any source or liquidate inventories of any size if the occasion demands.
> When he is in the process of negotiating a loan his sincere desire to render a service to business and his community is somewhat dwarfed by an even greater desire to insure recovery of the funds he passes out.
> It would not be too unjust to say that in the process of negotiating a loan the banker often exhibits a faint trace of skepticism which finds expression in vigorous demands for collateral, including everything from the borrower's life insurance down to his wife's gold teeth.[34]

But whatever the reason for the growing concern it was clear that there was far more agreement that pounce value was *not* an appropriate criterion than there was on what *was* an appropriate criterion. Sanders, Hatfield, and Moore attacked the pounce value concept:

> What is sometimes referred to among bankers as the "pouncing" value has no place in the balance-sheet of a company which probably will not be pounced upon for the satisfaction of its liabilities.[35]

But their ambivalence on the criterion that distinguishes current assets is clearly seen in their own definition of current assets:

> The current assets are those assets which in the regular course of business will be converted into cash and those assets acquired with a view to their availability for conversion into cash. No rule of thumb can be laid down for the precise separation of current assets from fixed assets, and frequently there are border-line items.[36]

One year later, Gilman echoed much the same thoughts:

> The simple distinction between current assets and fixed assets, while fundamental, is inadequate to meet modern accounting requirements.

---

34. Gilman, "Accounting Principles," pp. 112, 113.
35. Thomas Henry Sanders, Henry Rand Hatfield, and Underhill Moore, *A Statement of Accounting Principles* (New York: American Institute of Accountants, 1938), p. 3.
36. Sanders, Hatfield, and Moore, *Accounting Principles*, p. 70.

Certain kinds of assets cannot properly be classified as either current assets or fixed assets.[37]

Classification principles and practice became increasingly confused. Accountants agreed that current assets and liabilities should be identified on balance sheets but they did not agree on what a current asset was. Cash, trade receivables due within a year, and most inventories were nearly always classified as current but there was little agreement on precisely what those assets had in common. Without identifying a common element or criterion of classification accountants could not agree on how so-called "border-line" assets such as the cash surrender value of life insurance and prepaid items should be treated. Huizingh summarized the status of things as follows:

> By the dawn of the 1930s the concept of current assets, and hence of working capital, had undergone drastic modifications and had become a rather curious mixture of emphases on liquidity and circulation, on continuity and liquidation, on costs and realizable values. Wide variations in reporting practice were commonplace; competing views as to the composition of asset groups existed side by side in published statements.[38]

Development of ARB No. 30

In 1943 the committee on terminology, a committee of the American Institute of [Certified Public] Accountants which was "constituted" in 1940 "from the membership of the committee on accounting procedure," noted in its annual report that it had "given much consideration to the use of the term 'current assets' and 'current liabilities' " and had concluded that the "best approach to the problem would be to publish an extended discussion of the subject and invite comment thereon."[39]

Accordingly, Anson Herrick, one of the members of the committee, undertook the task, and the results were published in the January, 1944, issue of the *Journal of Accountancy* under the title, "Current Assets and Current Liabilities." That article deserves special

---

37. Stephen Gilman, *Accounting Concepts of Profit* (New York: Ronald Press, 1939), p. 261.
38. Huizingh, *Working Capital*, p. 93.
39. Accounting Research Bulletin no. 20 (Special), *Report of the Committee on Terminology* (New York: American Institute of [Certified Public] Accountants, 1943).

scrutiny for several reasons. First, it was, in effect, commissioned by the committee on terminology. Second, its author was a member of the committee on accounting procedure at the time Accounting Research Bulletin no. 30 was published, and he later took credit for "having been the one who developed the new concept" of working capital found in ARB no. 30.[40] That bulletin was later incorporated with only slight modification as chapter 3A of ARB no. 43 and remains in effect today.

Herrick's Views. Herrick's principal criticism of classification practice centered on the "one-year rule" used to identify both current assets and current liabilities. He described the rule as "arbitrary" and "inflexible" and claimed that it "stems back to a time when each year's business was looked upon in light of a separate venture, and overlooks the reduction in the usefulness of that concept." He further criticized the rule as misleading on the ground that "it is not logical to adopt a practice which may result in substantial difference between the reported amount of net current assets . . . and the amount which would be shown if the statement were to be prepared a few days earlier or later." To make matters worse, he argued that "the one-year rule is not consistently applied. The normal period of inventory frequently exceeds a year, yet it is customary to include the whole amount within the current category." He concluded his criticism of current practice with this observation:

> It is believed it should be clear that present practices do not rest upon a firm foundation; that they are not "draped over a firm theoretical skeleton so that they form a recognizable and logical body of thought," and consequently have become "unassorted and unrelated bodies of gaudy and drab material." It is believed equally clear that the finding of a firm foundation to support a logical body of practice would be a desirable accomplishment.[41]

Herrick saw the economists' distinction between fixed and circulating capital as the "firm foundation" that was needed and he saw the concept of the operating cycle as a means of implementing that distinction. He explained—

---

40. Anson Herrick, "A Review of the Work of the Accounting Procedure Committee," *Journal of Accountancy*, 98 (November, 1954): 627.
41. Anson Herrick, "Current Assets and Liabilities," *Journal of Accountancy*, 77 (January, 1944): 48 and 49.

> The capital of an enterprise consists of two parts—first, that which is invested or reserved for investment in the facilities *with which* to conduct its business. Second, that which is invested in the properties *in which* it deals, its working assets, or is held available for such use. Facilities (as the term is here used) comprise those assets which can be used over and over, though usually subject to a gradual wearing out, while working assets are available cash and those which are made to appear and disappear by the operations of the "operating cycle," a term here used to mean the series of transaction by which cash is exchanged (disbursed) for a commodity or service which in turn is exchanged (sold) for cash. . . . [The] term working capital is here used to mean the excess of the gross working capital, the total of quick and working assets, over the related or working liabilities.
>
> Working capital has a definite meaning and a significant relationship to total capital. Its determination leaves small room for variations of opinion and requires few arbitrary rules. It is believed to be the desired foundation.[42]

Later in the article, he defined current assets and current liabilities as follows:

> Those assets which are necessary or incidental to the operating cycle—exclusive of land and facilities—together with those assets which may be regarded as temporary investments of working capital and automatically will, or promptly can, be converted into free cash without impairing continuity and safety of operations.
>
> Those liabilities which are a natural consequence or incident of the operating cycle of an enterprise and, in effect, are liens upon current assets in that the funds for their liquidation are on hand, or will be obtained by realization upon existing current assets, indebtedness otherwise incurred which constitutes a withdrawal of working capital, and payments required to be made for long term debt liquidation installments to the extent that such have accrued.[43]

Opposition to Herrick. Although Herrick saw the economic distinction between fixed and circulating capital based on the concept of the operating cycle as a way out of both the arbitrariness and the inflexibility of the one-year rule, others had to be convinced. Herrick himself commented several years later that "Mr. Bailey and Mr. Blough, if I recall correctly, were the only two who were receptive to the concept that I proposed."[44] Nevertheless, a draft of what was

---

42. Herrick, "Current Assets and Liabilities," pp. 48 and 49.
43. Herrick, "Current Assets and Liabilities," pp. 50, 54, and 55.
44. Anson Herrick, "Comments by Anson Herrick," *Journal of Accountancy*, 110 (November, 1960): 50-51.

eventually to become ARB no. 30 was prepared following Herrick's article almost word for word with only slight modification and rearrangement of paragraphs. After reading this draft, Norman J. Lenhart, a prominent practitioner, commented as follows in a letter to the committee:

> It has always been my understanding and continues to be my understanding that the only reason for segregating "current" assets and liabilities is to give a reader of a statement information as to how likely it is that the concern can liquidate its indebtedness as such indebtedness comes due. To some degree I believe the proposed bulletin loses sight of what I understand is the reason for having a segregation of current assets and liabilities.

He went on to note that he could "see great confusion ahead in determining the 'operating cycle' of each line of business" and that he was "unable to find any logical basis set forth for determination of the liabilities which are to be included in current liabilities." Later in the letter he explained—

> I do not understand how you can make a test of currency of a liability on the basis of whether it constitutes "in effect, a lien against current assets." All liabilities, unless restricted, may be said to be, in effect, liens against existing current assets and other assets. If the test of the currency of a liability is whether it will be paid from "existing current assets, in the ordinary course of business" then I suppose that if current liabilities are $2,000,000 and current assets $1,000,000 then $1,000,000 of the current liabilities cannot be said to be current because obviously you cannot pay $2,000,000 of current liabilities out of $1,000,000 of current assets.

After three full pages of this type of criticism he closed with this comment:

> If you infer from the foregoing that I do not think much of the proposed statement you would be wrong. I really dislike it very much.

The Compromise. Others were also critical of Herrick's ideas and the proposed bulletin went through several revisions before it was finally adopted as ARB no. 30 by a surprising, unanimous vote of the committee on accounting procedure in August, 1947. Herrick himself later noted that although the bulletin, like all pronouncements of the committee on accounting procedure, "involved some compromise," the final bulletin "with one important and several minor exceptions, consisted of a full adoption of the originally proposed concept."[45]

Many of Herrick's ideas are obviously in the bulletin. His criticism of the one-year rule as well as his alternative to that rule, the operating cycle, are both present. Current assets are defined in terms of the operating cycle and Herrick's basic concept of a current liability as one that will be paid out of "existing current assets" rather than one due within a certain period of time is also present.

Some of the compromises Herrick referred to when he said the bulletin "involved some compromise" are not, however, minor matters of wording or detail. Some go to the very core of the subject matter of the bulletin and vitiate the ideas of Herrick that did find their way into the bulletin. For example, the basic definition of a current asset is followed by a statement that "a one-year time period is to be used as a basis for segregation of current assets in cases where there are several operating cycles occurring within such time period." Since most companies probably have an operating cycle of less than a year, this means that the "one-year rule" which Herrick had criticized so severely would still continue to be used for most companies. Similarly, the definition of current liabilities as those "the liquidation or payment of which is reasonably expected to require the use of existing resources properly classifiable as current assets or the creation of other current liabilities" is followed by the statement that: "other liabilities the regular and ordinary liquidation of which is expected to occur within a relatively short period of time, usually twelve months, are also intended for inclusion." Although Herrick may have believed the one-year rule was "arbitrary," "inflexible," and had outlived its usefulness, apparently other members of the committee were not so sure; at least, much of it was clearly left intact in ARB no. 30.

---

45. Herrick, "Comments by Herrick," p. 51.

4

Evaluation of Current-Noncurrent Classification Principles and Practices

Accounting Research Bulletin no. 30 issued by the committee on accounting procedure in 1947 is the only comprehensive pronouncement on current-noncurrent balance sheet classification ever issued by an authoritative body in the United States. In 1953 it was incorporated virtually unchanged as chapter 3A of Accounting Research Bulletin no. 43, a restatement and revision of the first forty-two bulletins issued by the committee. In that form, ARB no. 30 remains in effect today as the authoritative pronouncement of the U.S. accounting profession on the subject of current-noncurrent classification and provides the basis for present practice.

ARB no. 30 and practice based on it are evaluated in this chapter. This evaluation serves two purposes. First, it illustrates how little attention has been given to solvency issues in financial reporting. ARB no. 30 provides guidance on the principal reporting practice intended for solvency evaluation. A profession even mildly concerned with solvency could not have allowed a bulletin as defective as that one is to have remained in effect for over thirty years with no serious effort to change it. Second, it serves as a basis for the changes in present practice recommended in chapter 5.

Accounting Research Bulletin No. 30

The committee on accounting procedure intended that ARB no. 30 would provide a "firm foundation to support a logical body of practice," but the bulletin never achieved that objective. Many accountants resisted the application of some of its provisions almost from the day it was first approved. Eight months after it was issued, the editor of the *Journal of Accountancy* lamented:

> An example of the accountant's conservatism at its worst is the resistance of much of the profession to a recommendation of the American Institute of Accountants committee on accounting procedure, in Accounting Research Bulletin no. 30 that prepaid expenses be treated as current assets. Although this recommendation was unanimously adopted by the twenty-one distinguished members of the committee, it was greeted with cries of outraged indignation by many members of the profession who had always relied on the old rule of thumb that a current asset was something which would turn into cash within a year, or who had never given any thought to the matter.[1]

The recommendation that prepaid expenses be classified as current assets has received acceptance over the years, but overall the bulletin has not been successful. Classification practice today is described much as it was before the bulletin was issued, that is, as "inconsistent," "illogical," and "irrational."

Faulty Definitions. Current assets and current liabilities are both so poorly defined in the bulletin that it is often difficult if not impossible to determine whether a given asset or liability should be classified as current or noncurrent.

Current assets. Current assets are defined and described in the bulletin (paragraph 4) as follows:

> For accounting purposes, the term current assets is used to designate cash and other assets or resources commonly identified as those which are reasonably expected to be realized in cash or sold or consumed during the normal operating cycle of the business. Thus the term comprehends in general such resources as (a) cash available for current operations and items which are the equivalent of cash, (b) merchandise or stock on hand, or inventories of raw materials, goods in process,

---

1. "Prepaid Expenses as Current Assets," *Journal of Accountancy*, 85 (April, 1948): 273.

finished goods, operating supplies, and ordinary maintenance material and parts, (c) trade accounts, notes, and acceptances receivable, (d) receivables from officers (other than for loans and advances), employees, affiliates, and others if collectible in the ordinary course of business within a year, (e) installment or deferred accounts and notes receivable if they conform to normal trade practices and terms within the business, (f) marketable securities representing the investment of cash available for current operations, and (g) prepaid expenses such as insurance, taxes, unused royalties, current paid advertising service not yet received, and other items, which, if not paid in advance, would require the use of current assets during the operating cycle.

One of the problems with that definition is that the criterion "realized in cash or sold or consumed during the normal operating cycle" is excessively broad. At least a portion of nearly all assets will be "realized in cash or sold or consumed during the normal operating cycle." Thus, the authors of one leading accounting text argue that—

> In a realistic sense all asset services that will be used in producing revenue during the immediately succeeding operating cycle or accounting period will be realized and converted into liquid resources. Some portion of the investment in plant asset services will be realized in the same sense as will be the investment in raw materials. It may be argued, for example, that standing timber that will be manufactured into plywood in the next operating cycle has as good a claim to inclusion among current assets as a stock of glue that will bind the layers of wood.[2]

The concept of the operating cycle of a business is an integral part of the definition of current assets; to apply the definition, one

---

2. Walter B. Meigs, A. N. Mosich, and Charles E. Johnson, *Intermediate Accounting*, 4th ed. (New York: McGraw-Hill, 1978), p.144. For similar arguments, see Donald E. Kieso and Jerry J. Weygandt, *Intermediate Accounting* (New York: John Wiley, 1974), p.163; Saul Feldman, "A Critical Appraisal of the Current Asset Concept," *Accounting Review*, 34 (October, 1959): 574-578; Arthur Andersen & Co., *Accounting and Reporting Problems of the Accounting Profession*, 5th ed. (Chicago: Arthur Andersen & Co., 1976), p.185; and Eldon S. Hendriksen, *Accounting Theory*, 3d ed. (Homewood, Ill.: Richard D. Irwin, 1977), p. 295. Support for including next year's depreciation among current assets can also be found in Herrick's 1932 article, where he notes "depreciation or depletion to be deducted during the ensuing twelve months constitutes a sort of prepayment which might with propriety be included within current assets" (Anson Herrick, "What Should Be Included in Current Assets?" *Journal of Accountancy*, 53 (January, 1932): 58).

must first be able to determine the length of the operating cycle of an enterprise. The concept of the operating cycle, however, is also poorly defined. The bulletin (paragraph 5) states—

> The ordinary operations of a business involve a circulation of capital within the current asset group. Cash, when expended for materials, finished parts, operating supplies, labor and other factory services, is accumulated as inventory cost. Inventory costs, upon sale of the products to which such costs attach, are converted into trade receivables and ultimately into cash again. The average time intervening between the acquisition of materials or services entering this process and the final cash realization constitutes an "operating cycle." A one-year time period is to be used as a basis for the segregation of current assets in cases where there are several operating cycles occurring within such time period. However, where the period of the operating cycle is in excess of twelve months, such as in the tobacco, distillery, and lumber businesses, the longer period should be used.

Arthur Andersen & Co. pointed out some of the practical problems in determining the length of a company's operating cycle:

> A "circulation of capital with the current asset group" depends on a definition of what originates in that group. Why, in a manufacturing company, is a flow of cash to inventories (via payment for purchases, labor costs, and manufacturing costs) to receivables and back to cash an operating cycle any more than a flow of cash to manufacturing plant to inventories to receivables and back to cash?[3]

John W. Coughlan argued that the definitions of the operating cycle and of current assets "involve a complete circle" because "the operating cycle is defined as the time money is 'tied up' in current assets" and current assets are "defined as those that would be converted into cash within the operating cycle."[4] To illustrate his point, he used a numerical example involving a company that sells a portion of its output on open account with terms of forty-five days and a portion on installment terms payable over four and one-half years. He then reasoned —

> Consider the above attempt to determine whether installment receivables were current assets. Installment receivables were current if they

---

3. Arthur Andersen & Co., *Accounting and Reporting Problems*, pp. 185-86.
4. John W. Coughlan, "Working Capital and Credit Standing," *Journal of Accountancy*, 110 (November, 1960): 45.

would be realized in cash within the operating cycle; but whether they were so realized depended on whether they were included in the computation of this cycle. Installment receivables are a current asset if, in computing the normal operating cycle, *they are assumed to be current assets.*

In a similar manner, one could convert a steel plant, the Empire State Building, and any asset that has ever appeared on any balance sheet into a current asset. . . .

It may be argued, of course, that when accountants speak of current assets they are obviously not speaking about a steel plant or the Empire State Building . . . but these assets are excluded from the current category not because they differ from the definition but because by common agreement or assumption they are not considered current.[5]

Current liabilities. Current liabilities are defined and described in the bulletin (paragraph 7) as follows:

> The term current liabilities is used principally to identify and designate debts or obligations, the liquidation or payment of which is reasonably expected to require the use of existing resources properly classifiable as current assets or the creation of other current liabilities. As a balance-sheet category, the classification is intended to include obligations for items which have entered into the operating cycle, as in the case of payables incurred in the aquisition of materials and supplies to be used in the production of goods or in providing services to be offered for sale, collections received in advance of the delivery of goods or performance of services, and debts which arise from operations directly related to the operating cycle, such as accruals for wages, salaries, commissions, rentals, or royalties. Other liabilities the regular and ordinary liquidation of which is expected to occur within a relatively short period of time, usually twelve months, are also intended for inclusion, such as short-term debts arising from the aquisition of capital assets, serial maturities of long-term obligations, and agency obligations arising from the collection or acceptance of cash or other assets for the account of a third party. Income taxes should be included as current liabilities even though the entire amount may not be payable within twelve months. [Footnotes omitted]

The principal deficiency of that definition is that it is based on an assumed relationship between specific assets and specific liabilities that does not exist. Most liabilities are paid with cash and most cash is received from collecting receivables that arise from sale of a company's products, merchandise, or services to its customers. As pointed out in chapter 2, it is meaningless to try to determine which

---

5. Coughlan, "Working Capital," pp. 45-46 (emphasis original).

of a company's many assets were the source of the cash used to pay a particular liability; receivables, inventory, prepaid expenses, plant, equipment, and furniture and fixtures are all used in conjuntion with one another to generate cash. Similarly, it is meaningless to try to determine which of a company's liabilities "is reasonably expected to require the use of existing resources properly classifiable as current assets." To try to do so is a futile exercise. Or, as Coughlan put it,

> The endless, continual inflows and outflows of cash are all related and no manner of definition is going to establish a unique and single relationship between one expenditure and one receipt any more than it will be possible to find the one strand in the spider's web that caught the fly.[6]

Some accountants have interpreted the phrase "require the use of existing resources properly classifiable as current assets" to mean that the length of a company's operating cycle should be used to classify its current liabilities as well as its current assets. Paul Grady, for example, stated—

> Current liabilities should include items payable within one year or at the end of the operating cycle used in the classification of current assets.[7]

Robert E. Seiler interpreted the definition similarly:

> When the operating cycle exceeds 12 months, the company's current liabilities include those payable within the next cycle.[8]

In practice most liabilities due after one year are classified as noncurrent even if a company uses an operating cycle of several years' duration in classifying current assets. The point here is not whether Grady and Seiler's interpretation or that usually followed in practice is correct; the point is that the definition is ambiguous—it is subject to disparate interpretations because its application requires

---

6. Coughlan, "Working Capital," p.44.
7. Paul Grady, *Inventory of Generally Accepted Accounting Principles for Business Enterprises*, Accounting Research Study no. 7 (New York: American Institute of Certified Public Accountants, 1965), p. 277.
8. Robert E. Seiler, "Current Liabilities," chap. 21 in *Handbook of Modern Accounting*, ed. Sidney Davidson (New York: McGraw-Hill, 1970), pp.21-23.

accountants to trace a relationship between specific liabilities and specific assets that does not exist.

Itemized lists. The basic definitions of both current assets and current liabilities in the bulletin are followed by itemized lists of specific assets and liabilities that should be either included in or excluded from the current category. Those lists have only served to confuse further the concepts of current assets and current liabilities that the committee sought to implement. Some of the assets that the bulletin states should be classified as current do not fit the bulletin's definition of a current asset. For example, installment receivables are required to be classified as current "if they conform to trade practices and terms within the business," not if they "are reasonably expected to be realized in cash or sold or consumed during the normal operating cycle."[9] Similarly, receivables from "officers, employees, affiliates, and others" are to be classified as current only "if collectible in the ordinary course of business within a year" regardless of how long a company's operating cycle may be. Prepaid expenses are declared to be current "not . . . in the sense that they will be converted into cash but in the sense that, if not paid in advance, they would require the use of current assets during the operating cycle."

The list of liabilities that the bulletin requires to be classified as current has also been the source of confusion. Herrick believed that installment payments due within the next year should not be classified as current if they were to be paid from "funds realized through depreciation or depletion," and he apparently felt that the definition of current liabilities excluded them. In the 1944 article previously cited, he stated—

> Where . . . retirement installments are contemplated to be met out of funds realized through depreciation or depletion . . . the inclusion in current liabilities of all debt installments due within a year is wholly unwarranted.[10]

---

9. Herrick stated in 1960 that these words "never should have appeared" in the bulletin because "Manifestly accounting principles are not determined by a trade practice" (Anson Herrick, "Comments by Anson Herrick," *Journal of Accountancy*, 110 (November, 1960): 52).
10. Anson Herrick, "Current Assets and Liabilities," *Journal of Accountancy*, 77 (January, 1944): 54.

In 1960, he lamented—

> Unfortunately the bulletin has not had the expected liberal and logical interpretation but has been strictly interpreted as requiring . . . the inclusion as a current liability of debt installments notwithstanding that there was a clear and normal relationship between the debt installments and the prospective natural resource or depreciation recovery. Such relationship becomes quite obvious where the installment is measured by depletion recovery, as in timber, or where the installments are calculated to approximate the depreciation recovery as in the case of debt created in the aquisition of motor trucks.
>
> If the bulletin were to be reasonably and logically interpreted, consistent with its underlying philosophy, the understatement of working capital [from classifying installment debt due within one year as current] would not exist.[11]

Undoubtedly some of those who "strictly interpreted" the bulletin did so because the sentence following the basic definition states categorically that "serial maturities of long-term obligations" which are to be liquidated "within a relatively short period of time" should be included in current liabilities.

Ironically, the lists of balance sheet items that are to be included in or excluded from the current category are probably the most useful feature of the bulletin. They have undoubtedly provided a uniformity to classification practice that would not have been achieved without them. However, because the reasons for including certain items and excluding others are not apparent and because designation of many items conflicts with the basic definitions, they are also the source of criticism that classification practice is "inconsistent," "illogical," and "irrational."

Some of the accountants interviewed in the course of this study argued that a precise definition of current assets is unimportant, that the important point is that current assets are the relatively liquid ones, and it does not matter exactly where the line is drawn. That argument, however, does not answer the criticism expressed here. As pointed out in chapter 1, the term liquidity is used in at least two different ways. It lacks analytical precision. Defining current assets in terms of "relatively liquid" assets merely moves the definitional problem back one step. A meaningful definition of current assets in terms of relative liquidity requires that relative liquidity first be defined in operational terms, such as assets that will be converted into cash within a year or assets that will be consumed during the next operat-

---

11. Herrick, "Comments by Herrick," p. 51.

ing cycle. That, of course, is what is lacking, and defining current assets in terms of relative liquidity therefore adds no meaning at all to the term current assets.

Evaluation of Underlying Concepts. Some of the defects in the definitions of current assets and current liabilities and the conflicts between the definitions and the lists of assets and liabilities are undoubtedly due to what Anson Herrick later referred to as "compromises with a diehard to whom a year collection period was truly a sacred cow," but the deficiencies of the bulletin are more fundamental than that.[12] The underlying concepts and reasoning on which the bulletin is built are also defective. Before analyzing those underlying issues, a number of basic concepts of classification used in this as well as subsequent sections need to be introduced.

Basic concepts of classification. Classification is a purposive human activity; all items, concepts, and events have an unlimited number of properties or attributes that may be used as a basis of classification. As Raymond J. Chambers observed,

> Objects *may* be classified only if they are perceived to have some property in common. Objects *will* be classified only if classification promotes the attainment of some purpose.[13]

That line of reasoning is central in the analysis of balance sheet classification. Assets and liabilities have an unlimited number of attributes including, for example, method of valuation, due date, legal enforceability, period of time that will normally elapse until conversion into cash, amount of cash that would be realized in forced conversion, source, geographical location, date recorded in the accounts, and so forth. Any of these *may* be used as a basis of classification. Which, if any, of them *should* be used in classifying assets and liabilities as current or noncurrent or as anything else depends on the objective of balance sheet classification.

An obvious corollary of the purposive nature of classification is that there are no natural classes of things. Even if a group of items or objects contains common attributes that can be used to differentiate them from other similar items, assigning a separate name to that

---

12. Herrick, "Comments by Herrick," p. 52.
13. Raymond J. Chambers, *Accounting, Evaluation and Economic Behavior* (Englewood Cliffs, N.J.: Prentice-Hall, 1966), p. 85 (emphasis original).

group is unnecessary if no useful purpose is served in doing so. Thus, if no useful purpose is served by assigning the name "current" to subgroups of assets and liabilities, that practice should be abandoned; it is inherent neither in the nature of assets and liabilities nor in the accounting process.

A second corollary of the purposive nature of classification is that definitions are not "true" in the sense that they are inherent in the nature of things. A definition is simply a means of identifying the partitioning attribute or attributes of a class of items, concepts, qualities, or events.

A definition that identifies the partitioning attributes used to determine whether a given item is included in or excluded from the class "current assets" cannot be proved right or wrong on the basis of logic; it can only be evaluated as more or less useful for a given objective than an alternative basis of classification.

A third corollary of the purposive nature of classification is that definitions are transitory; as the needs of society change, definitions must be changed to meet those new needs.

The controversy now going on over the definition of death illustrates this point. Death of a human being used to be defined in terms of cessation of heartbeat and respiration. Those criteria were considered adequate for all purposes for which a definition of death was needed. Several years ago, however, society began to question whether a definition based on those criteria was appropriate for deciding when a vital human organ may be removed for transplant to another person since medical technology now makes it possible, at least in some cases, to maintain some functions of a person's body almost indefinitely even though it is virtually certain that consciousness will never be regained.[14] The objective of deciding when a vital human organ may be removed for transplant gave rise to a need for a new definition of death. The American Bar Association, through the Uniform Law Commission, has therefore recommended that a new definition of death based on cessation of brain function rather than cessation of heartbeat and respiration be adopted.[15]

---

14. Richard B. James, "Doctors Debate: What is Life?" *Wall Street Journal*, July 27, 1970.
15. Edward Edelson, "When You're Dead, You're Dead (?)" *Seattle Times*, April 27, 1975.

S. I. Hayakawa, the semanticist, observed—

> What we call things and where we draw the line between one class of things and another depend upon the interest we have and the purpose of the classification.
>
> Classification is not a matter of identifying "essences" as is widely believed. It is simply a reflection of social convenience and necessity—and different necessities are always producing different classifications.[16]

The term, "current assets," like the term "death," has no "true" meaning independent of the purpose to be served in defining current assets. The term can be defined for financial reporting in many different ways. Searching for the "true" definition of current assets or a definition that identifies the "essence," the "substance," or the "fundamental characteristic" of current assets can only lead to confusion and ultimately to failure.

In the discussion that follows, the primary objective of classifying assets and liabilities as current or noncurrent is assumed to be that of providing information useful in evaluating a company's solvency. Although that objective has often been ignored, whenever the issue has been raised there is substantial agreement that that is an appropriate objective and the one accountants have sought to achieve by classification. ARB no. 30 begins with the statement "The working capital of a borrower has always been of prime interest to grantors of credit," and Leopold A. Bernstein noted that "The popularity of working capital as a measure of liquidity and of short-term financial help is so widespread that it hardly needs documentation."[17]

Fixed and circulating capital. As noted in chapter 3, Herrick's ideas about working capital had their roots in the distinction between fixed and circulating capital developed by 18th and 19th century economists. In fact, shortly after ARB no. 30 was issued, Carman Blough commented—

> In attempting to refine the classification of working capital one should recognize that the Committee was trying to put into practice a distinc-

---

16. S. I. Hayakawa, *Language in Thought and Action*, 2d ed. (New York: Harcourt, Brace and World, 1964), pp. 215 and 217.
17. Leopold A. Bernstein, *Financial Statement Analysis*, rev. ed. (Homewood, Ill.: Richard D. Irwin, 1978), p. 447.

tion drawn by economists for decades [centuries], namely, a distinction between capital which has reached its final use and that which is still circulating or in process of exchange.[18]

Adam Smith, John Stuart Mill, and other 18th and 19th century economists were concerned with explaining how a competitive economy worked. They were concerned with how prices were determined, how the relative productivities of the economies of different countries were determined, what factors determined the distribution of income, and similar issues. The concept of capital was central to much of their discussion and they found it useful to distinguish between fixed and circulating capital. They wanted to emphasize that the term capital embraced not only the obvious tools of the trade used in physical production (fixed capital) but also cash, inventory, and so forth (circulating capital) which, although not as obvious, is nevertheless just as necessary for the conduct of business as fixed capital.

The distinction between fixed and circulating capital was also used by early economists for other purposes. Smith, for example, argued that when calculating national income (or what he called "the neat revenue of the society") "though the whole expense of maintaining fixed capital is thus necessarily excluded . . . it is not the same case with that of maintaining the circulating capital."[19] Mill felt the distinction was significant in determining the level of employment and argued that "all increase of fixed capital, when taking place at the expense of circulating, must be, at least temporarily, prejudicial to the interests of the laborers."[20]

It is not necessary to discuss the merits of those arguments here, because the only point relevant to this discussion is that when those writers distinguished between fixed and circulating capital, they were clearly not thinking of financial statement users' needs for information useful in evaluating solvency. Their purpose in developing that distinction was not to provide information to those users. If balance sheet classification based on that distinction does happen to be useful to investors, creditors, and other users, it is clearly a matter of acci-

---

18. Carman G. Blough, "Classification of Prepaid Expenses as Current Assets," *Robert Morris Associates Bulletin*, February, 1948, p. 353.
19. Adam Smith, *The Wealth of Nations* (New York: Random House, 1937), p. 272.
20. John Stuart Mill, *Principles of Political Economy*, rev. ed. (New York: Colonial Press, 1899), p. 93.

dent and not of design. The distinction should not have been implanted in accounting as the basis of balance sheet classification merely because early economists found it useful for their purposes. If its utility for evaluating solvency cannot be sustained it should not be used as the balance sheet classification.[21]

Unfortunately, Anson Herrick, the principal architect of ARB no. 30, provided little insight into why he felt that balance sheet classification based on the fixed-circulating distinction would be useful. Nearly all of his arguments were directed to pointing out that the one-year rule is *not* an appropriate basis of classification rather than to explaining why the fixed-circulating distinction *would be* useful. He apparently believed that if he could establish the inappropriateness of the one-year rule, the case for the fixed-circulating distinction would be made. He believed his approach would result in showing "true " working capital; application of the one-year rule resulted in what he described as "erroneous" or "incorrect" measures:

> As the bulletin . . . indicates, it was believed that the existing procedures for the determination of working capital were arbitrary, inconsistent, and frequently did not result in the development of a *true* amount of working capital and, accordingly, it would be desirable for procedures to be provided which would do so. There was no thought that the committee was doing anything other than developing a more logical concept of working capital which, because *more accurate*, would be more useful.[22]

That argument is not only unconvincing, but also revealing; it highlights the inattention to an essential element of an attempt to

---

21. Littleton questioned the relevance to accounting of Adam Smith's distinction between fixed and circulating capital as early as 1938. He commented, "Management may also have been innocently misled by an outmoded tradition, inherited by our accounting literature from certain early British ideas and never thoroughly examined, to the effect that there was something in a business by the name of capital assets in which losses or gains could be recognized as quite distinct from other asset changes called expenses and revenues. Probably the tradition runs back to the double-account balance sheet prescribed for British railroad companies in 1868 and to the theory of plant maintenance, in place of depreciation allowances, which was so solidly entrenched in railroad practice. Possibly both ideas derive from an interpretation of Adam Smith's observation of fixed and circulating capital which, no doubt, was based on conceptions related more to landed estates than to business enterprises" (A.C. Littleton, "High Standards of Accounting," *Journal of Accountancy* 66 (August, 1938); 101).
22. Herrick, "Comments by Herrick," p. 52 (emphasis supplied).

improve balance sheet classification, which is the purpose of the classification. Using Herrick's approach, only by sheer chance could the committee's efforts have been expected to result in improved information to financial statement users.

Operating cycle. The operating cycle was a key concept in Herrick's ideas, particularly in his 1944 article. He defined both current assets and current liabilities in terms of it and he referred to it throughout his writings. He was not precise about what he meant by the operating cycle; he defined it only parenthetically as "disbursement of cash for merchandise, its sale, and the recovery thereby of the originally ventured cash and profit to boot."[23] More important, he did not explain why its length should be such a key element in identifying current assets.

A company's operating cycle could, of course, be defined in operational terms to eliminate the confusion that now exists in practice over how the length of an operating cycle should be measured. No reason, however, is apparent as to why the operating cycle should be a classification criterion at all. Managers plan and think in terms of calendar periods—weeks, quarters, or years—not operating cycles, because most companies operate continuously (with perhaps seasonal fluctuations), rather than in discrete cycles. The things that influence the length of a company's operating cycle, such as the length of the credit terms it offers its customers and the length of its manufacturing process, also influence the *amount* of receivables and inventory it must carry. It does not follow, however, that the length of its operating cycle has any relevance in determining whether its receivables and inventory should be classified as current or noncurrent for the purpose of helping financial statement users evaluate a company's solvency. Perhaps the underlying reason for introducing the operating cycle is that it provided a rationale for avoiding the difficult problem of estimating when a company's inventory will be sold, a judgment that would have to be made if a fixed time period such as a year were to be applied consistently to all assets.

Herrick's recommendation that the length of a company's operating cycle be used in classifying its assets and liabilities has received little attention or support in accounting literature. Colin Park and John W. Gladson are among the few who have written on the topic. They argue as follows:

---

23. Herrick, "Current Assets and Liabilities," p. 48.

While the notion of one-year currentness may have been an inadvertently useful rule of thumb, it fails to mould accountancy toward operational time. Thus the statement of the American Institute Committee on Accounting Procedure is in several respects a forward step toward realism in the accounting-period concept. It challenges accountancy to get away from arbitrariness in measures of currentness. The shortcoming of the pronouncement is its inconsistency: ". . . where the period of the operating cycle is more than twelve months . . . , the longer period is to be used," but "a one-year time period is to be used . . . where there are several operating cycles occurring within a year." This is a one-way rule that scarcely changes the old one-year currentness guide for financial statement construction.

Whether the length of the operating cycle in a given situation is determined to be greater *or less* than 12 months, the operating cycle is the criterion for currentness that should apply in constructing figures for financial planning and control. If, as a result of applying the arbitrary one-year criterion, working capital is incorrectly measured, the lure of free-capital commitment beyond the real liquidity potential of an enterprise may not be seen.[24]

Writing alone, Park later argued—

When working capital balances, inflows, and outflows, are oriented to the operating cycle of a business, the arbitrary, artificial, conventional one-year concept of enterprise free capital must give way to realism.[25]

These arguments are similar to those of Herrick and are unconvincing for the same reason. The case for the operating cycle as a classification criterion cannot successfully be made by arguing that the one-year rule is "arbitrary," "artificial," and "conventional" and results in an "incorrect" measure of working capital while the operating cycle "gives way to realism" and shows the "lure of free-capital commitment beyond the real liquidity potential of an enterprise." These arguments are meaningless because they ignore the purpose of classification.

Usefulness of Current Practice

There are three basic ways that balance sheet classification of assets and liabilities as current or noncurrent might be useful in evaluating a

---

24. Colin Park and John W. Gladson, *Working Capital* (New York: Macmillan, 1963), pp. 33-35 (emphasis original).
25. Colin Park, "Funds Flow," chap. 14 in *Modern Accounting Theory*, ed. Morton Backer (Englewood Cliffs, N.J.: Prentice-Hall, 1966), p. 310.

company's solvency. First, it might be useful as a means of disclosing an important attribute or characteristic of assets and liabilities. If, for example, classification of an asset as current meant that it would be converted into cash within a certain period of time, classification would be useful because when an asset will be converted into cash is an attribute that is relevant in estimating the future cash flows of a company and future cash flows are relevant to the evaluation of a company's solvency. Classification is used as a way of disclosing attributes of items in many areas.

Second, classification might be useful in predicting financial failure through the use of ratios. Thus, even if classification provides financial statement users with no knowledge of the attributes of assets and liabilities, it might still be useful if ratios based on the information provided by the classification bear a predictable relationship to financial failure. The current ratio, in other words, might be associated with a company's ability to pay its debts when due even though at present there may be no accepted theory that explains that relationship. If that is true, it might be argued that classification of assets and liabilities as current or noncurrent is useful simply because it helps predict financial failure.

There is also a third way that current classification practice might be useful. Even if it were found that ratios based on that classification do not actually predict financial failure or that they are poor predictors of financial failure, it might still be argued that if financial statement users do, in fact, calculate current and other ratios that require assets and liabilities to be classified, the practice of having accountants designate which assets and liabilities they believe should be called current is useful because it spares users the need to do their own classification.

Current classification practice is discussed and evaluated in the light of all three of these concepts of usefulness in this section.

Attribute Disclosure. It was noted in the introduction to this chapter that balance sheet classification practice today is described in much the same way it was before ARB no. 30 was issued—as inconsistent, illogical, and irrational. Philip E. Fess, for example, described the "inconsistency in the inclusion of a three-year prepaid insurance premium . . . as a current asset while excluding machinery and equipment having a three-year life" and went on to argue that—

CHAPTER 4: CURRENT-NONCURRENT CLASSIFICATION PRINCIPLES

In terms of the influence on both liquidity and flow of funds, there appears to be no significant basis for distinguishing between the two acquisitions.[26]

Arthur Andersen & Co.'s discussion of the working capital "problem" begins with the following comment:

> Working-capital classifications are more the result of custom than logic, and various practices have evolved over the years. A serious question exists concerning whether there is any proper basis for many of these customs that are followed in actual practice.

The logic of current classification practice is then implicitly criticized by asking a series of rhetorical questions:

> Why should crude oil inventories in tanks be considered current assets, but the cost of oil reserves in the ground that are to be produced within one year be considered noncurrent assets? Likewise, should gas stored in underground reserves to be produced in one year be treated as a noncurrent asset?
>
> In a mining company, why should maintenance supplies and parts that ordinarily turn over during a period of three or more years be included in current assets, while deferred stripping and development costs to be amortized over a similar period as the minerals are produced are included in noncurrent assets?
>
> Why should significant amounts of materials and supplies be carried as current assets in some industries when they are transferred to noncurrent property accounts upon the usage for which they are intended?[27]

Huizingh used different words to express his views of current practice, but his message was the same:

> Irrationalities in practice abound. Inventories are classed as current even though it is anticipated that they will be sold to installment buyers, and that the resulting receivable will not qualify as a current asset. Certain materials and supplies are deemed current despite the fact that their cost will attach to property accounts upon being used as intended. The entire cost of prepayments is regarded as current, whereas the entire cost of a productive asset with a similar life expectancy is consid-

---

26. Philip E. Fess, "The Working Capital Concept," *Accounting Review*, 41 (April, 1966): 267.
27. Arthur Andersen & Co., *Accounting and Reporting Problems*, pp. 181 and 186.

ered fixed. The next year's portion of long term debt incurred to acquire wasting assets is treated as a current liability, but the cost of the asset to be recovered from next year's operations is denied current status even though there is an obvious relationship between them, and the terms of the loan agreement may provide for debt retirement based on the asset recovery.

Much additional evidence of inconsistency could be adduced, but the instances presented suffice to establish that existing practice is far from rational.[28]

The basic point that these authors are making is that current practice fails to communicate information about the attributes of assets and liabilities effectively. A prerequisite of effective communication through classification is that all items classified the same way have some attribute in common—the attribute used as the criterion to partition the items into classes. A user of classified data then knows that if an item is classified in a certain way, it possesses a certain attribute. Communication of attributes is one of the principal functions of nearly all forms of classification. When Fess refers to the "inconsistency" of classifying a three-year prepaid insurance premium as current while machinery with a three-year life is classified as noncurrent, he is really saying that there is no partitioning attribute that a three-year prepaid insurance premium has in common with other assets classified as current but that machinery with a three-year life does not have. When Arthur Andersen & Co. questions the "logic" of classifying crude oil inventories in tanks while similar underground reserves are classified as noncurrent, it is really saying that there is no partitioning attribute that crude oil inventories in tanks have in common with other assets classified as current but that underground reserves do not have. When Huizingh labels as "irrational" and "inconsistent" the practice of classifying materials and supplies that will be used to maintain fixed assets as current, while the fixed assets themselves are classified as noncurrent, he is really saying that there is no partitioning attribute that spare parts inventories and supplies have in common with other assets classified as current but that fixed assets do not have.

The effect of classifying assets in these "inconsistent," "illogical," and "irrational" ways is that describing an asset as current communicates no useful information about that asset to financial statement

---

28. William Huizingh, *Working Capital Classification* (Ann Arbor, Mich.: University of Michigan, 1967), p.107.

users because there is no identifiable attribute that all assets classified as current have but all assets classified as noncurrent do not have. The concept of current assets found in practice cannot be described as "those assets that will normally be converted into cash within a year," because many assets that will not be converted into cash within a year are classified as current while others with the same attribute are classified as noncurrent; they cannot be described as assets "reasonably expected to be realized in cash or sold or consumed during the normal operating cycle" because many assets that will be "realized in cash or sold or consumed" during the next operating cycle (whatever its length) such as a portion of plant and equipment and wasting assets, are excluded; they cannot be described as resources that will be used to pay liabilities classified as current because cash generated from the use of all assets is used to pay both liabilities classified as current as well as those classified as noncurrent. The only attribute that all assets classified as current have in common is that they are the assets that, under current accepted practice, are classified as current—an attribute that has no information content whatever to a user of financial statements concerned with evaluating the solvency of a business enterprise. This same basic criticism applies equally to current practice in classifying liabilities. A current liability can only be described as a liability that is classified as current.

A second prerequisite to effective communication of attributes through classification of data is that the user of classified data know what attribute was used to partition the data. If a user believes that one attribute was used when a different one was used, classification is not merely useless, it is pernicious; it does not just fail to disclose relevant attributes of assets and liabilities, it misleads users of that data.

Many classification rules followed in practice undoubtedly mislead financial statement users because users believe that accountants classify assets and liabilities on the basis of one attribute when, in fact, they use an entirely different criterion. An example is the failure to disclose the length of a company's operating cycle. According to some accounting practitioners, the operating cycles used to classify assets in some companies may be ten or more years. It seems likely that many users, even sophisticated ones, are misled by the practice of classifying receivables due five or more years hence as current because they think of current assets as ones that will normally be converted into cash in the short run. They are unaware of the long operating cycles used as classification criteria for some companies.

There are many other classification practices that undoubtedly mislead users. For example, users who think that current assets are "cash and other assets that are reasonably expected to be realized in cash or sold or consumed during the normal operating cycle of the business or within one year if the operating cycle is shorter than one year" are no doubt misled by the common practice of classifying a three-year prepaid insurance premium as a current asset even though the operating cycle of the insured is less than one year.[29] They are undoubtedly also misled by the classification of underground oil reserves that are "reasonably expected to be . . . sold . . . within one year" as *noncurrent* assets.

Perhaps the most misleading information produced by current classification practice is the classification of deferred income tax debits and credits. Deferred income tax credits, for example, are classified as current on the basis of whether they "relate" to current assets, not on the basis of when they are expected to "reverse" or require the use of cash.[30] It seems likely that many financial statement users believe that current deferred taxes will have to be paid or will "reverse" within a relatively short period of time such as a year, because the one-year rule is followed quite closely in classifying most liabilities. Actually, however, when they will have to be paid or when they "reverse" has nothing to do with how they are classified, and in many, if not most, situations there probably is no basis for assuming they will have to be paid or will "reverse" sooner than even those deferred tax credits classified as noncurrent.

To summarize, present classification is not useful as a means of disclosing an important attribute or characteristic of assets and liabilities. And furthermore, it is misleading because the attributes used to partition currrent from noncurrent assets and liabilities are not clearly identified, are not understood by users, and are not followed consistently in practice.

Prediction of Financial Failure. One approach to evaluating the usefulness of financial information is to measure its ability to predict the outcome of future events.[31] This approach has been used by

---

29. APB Statement no. 4, par. 25.
30. Paragraph 56 of APB Opinion no. 11 provides that "the current portions of (deferred tax charges and credits) should be those amounts which related to assets and liabilities classified as current."
31. For a discussion of this approach, see William H. Beaver, John W. Kennelly, and William M. Voss, "Predictive Ability as a Criterion for the Evaluation of Accounting Data," *Accounting Review*, 43 (October, 1968): 675-683.

several researchers in recent years to evaluate the usefulness of financial ratios in predicting financial failure.[32] Perhaps the best known of those studies and the ones most relevant to this study are those by William H. Beaver.[33]

Beaver's data base for both studies consisted of a paired sample of seventy-nine firms that failed and a similar number of comparable firms that did not fail. In his first study he examined thirty financial ratios. His general findings were as follows:

> Based solely upon a knowledge of the financial ratios, the failure status of firms can be correctly predicted to a much greater extent than would be expected from random prediction. For example, one year before failure the cash flow to total debt ratio misclassified only 13 percent of the sample firms. Five years before failure the same ratio misclassified only 22 percent. Since there was approximately an equal number of failed and nonfailed firms in the sample, the expected error from random prediction was about 50 percent. There is an extremely small probability that random prediction could have done as well as the ratio.
>
> This evidence, together with other tests conducted, suggested that financial ratios can be useful in the prediction of failure for at least five years prior to the event.[34]

In his second study, Beaver examined the difference in predictive power of fourteen different ratios divided into two groups: those described as liquid asset ratios and those described as nonliquid asset ratios. Those ratios are identified in the table below. The eleven liquid asset ratios all relate some measure of assets described as liquid to total assets, to current liabilities, or to sales. Seven of them are based on current assets, current liabilities, or working capital, all of which depend on current-noncurrent classifications. The three nonliquid asset ratios studied were cash flow to total debt, net income to total debt, and total debt to total assets—none of which depend on current-noncurrent classification. According to Beaver, the nonliquid ratios studied were selected "because they predicted best among the

---

32. For discussion and citations of these studies, see Baruch Lev, *Financial Statement Analysis: A New Approach* (Englewood Cliffs, N. J.: Prentice-Hall, 1974), chap 9.
33. William H. Beaver, "Financial Ratios as Predictors of Failure," *Empirical Research in Accounting, Selected Studies*, 1966, supplement to vol. 4, *Journal of Accounting Research*, pp. 71-127; and "Alternative Accounting Measures as Predictors of Failure," *Accounting Review*, 43 (January, 1968): 113-122.
34. Beaver, "Alternative Measures," p. 114.

nonliquid asset ratios in the earlier study."[35] Beaver summarized the findings of his second study as follows:

> The most striking feature of the data is the consistently superior performance of the nonliquid asset ratios. . . . No single liquid asset ratio predicts as well as any of the nonliquid asset ratios.
> Surprisingly, the superior predictive power exists not only in the long term but also in the years shortly before failure. . . .[36]

Table 4-1

Ratios Used in Beaver Study

I. Nonliquid asset ratios
  1. Cash flow to total debt
  2. Net income to total assets
  3. Total debt to total assets

II. Liquid asset ratios
A. Total Asset Group
  1. Current assets to total assets
  2. Quick assets to total assets
  3. Net working capital to total assets
  4. Cash to total assets

II. Liquid asset ratios
B. Current Debt Group
  1. Current assets to current debt (current ratio)
  2. Quick assets to current debt (quick ratio)
  3. Cash to current debt
C. Net Sales or Turnover Group
  1. Current assets to sales
  2. Quick assets to sales
  3. Net working capital to sales
  4. Cash to sales

Beaver was not specifically concerned with the usefulness of current-noncurrent classification. He did not, therefore, comment on the relative predictive power of ratios based on that classification compared with those not based on it, but his article does contain data showing the predictive power of each of the ratios studied for each of the five years before failure. That data is reproduced in the table on page 65.

---

35. Beaver, "Alternative Measures," p. 114n.
36. Beaver, "Alternative Measures," p. 117.

Table 4-2

Percentage Error for 14 Ratios on Dichotomous Classification Test

Ratio	_5_	_4_	_3_	_2_	_1_	Average for 5 years*
Nonliquid asset group						
$\dfrac{\text{Cash flow}}{\text{Total debt}}$	22	24	23	21	13	21
$\dfrac{\text{Net Income}}{\text{Total assets}}$	28	29	23	21	13	23
$\dfrac{\text{Total debt}}{\text{Total assets}}$	28	27	34	25	19	27
Liquid asset to total asset group						
$\dfrac{\text{Current assets}}{\text{Total assets}}$	49	47	48	48	38	46.0
$\dfrac{\text{Quick assets}}{\text{Total assets}}$	40	48	36	42	38	41
$\dfrac{\text{Working capital}}{\text{Total assets}}$	41	45	33	34	24	35
$\dfrac{\text{Cash}}{\text{Total assets}}$	38	36	30	29	28	32
Liquid asset to current debt group						
$\dfrac{\text{Current assets}}{\text{Current liabilities}}$	45	38	36	32	20	34
$\dfrac{\text{Quick assets}}{\text{Current liabilities}}$	37	34	40	32	24	33
$\dfrac{\text{Cash}}{\text{Current liabilities}}$	38	38	36	28	22	32

*This column represents the author's calculations.

Table 4-2 *(continued)*

Percentage Error for 14 Ratios on Dichotomous Classification Test

Ratio	Year before failure					Average for 5 years*
	5	4	3	2	1	
Liquid asset turnover group						
$\dfrac{\text{Current assets}}{\text{Sales}}$	51	49	48	51	44	49
$\dfrac{\text{Quick assets}}{\text{Sales}}$	44	52	45	47	46	47
$\dfrac{\text{Working capital}}{\text{Sales}}$	40	46	42	33	26	38
$\dfrac{\text{Cash}}{\text{Sales}}$	45	43	36	24	34	36

SOURCE: William H. Beaver, "Alternative Accounting Measures as Predictors of Failure," *The Accounting Review*, January, 1968, p. 118.

*This column represents the author's calculations.

In general, those data show that the ratios based on current-noncurrent classification are not only poorer predictors of financial failure than the three nonliquid asset ratios he studied, but, within the liquid asset group itself, they are among the poorer predictors. The current ratio was found to have the poorest average predictive power of the three ratios of liquid assets to current debt and, except for the year immediately before failure, was a poorer predictor than the ratio of just plain cash to total assets. The ratio of current assets to total assets had the poorest average predictive power of the four ratios of liquid assets to total assets, and the ratio of current assets to sales had the poorest average predictive power of the four ratios of liquid assets to sales (liquid asset turnover group).

Although Beaver's findings are of interest here, there are at least two reasons why they do not support the hypothesis that accountants should continue classification of assets and liabilities as current or noncurrent on the grounds that that practice is necessary to enable financial statement users to calculate ratios which are particularly useful in predicting financial failure. First, Beaver, did not find that ratios based on current-noncurrent classification are particularly useful in predicting financial failure. He found that those ratios have relatively poor predictive power. Second, even if ratios based on current-noncurrent classification were found to be among the most useful in predicting financial failure, it would not necessarily follow that *accountants* should designate which assets and liabilities they believe should be classified as current. Beaver found that "Quick assets . . . is a better predictor than current assets" yet accountants do not designate which assets they believe are "quick." That classification is left to users. Balance sheet classification by accountants is not a prerequisite to the use of current and other predictive ratios based on groupings of assets and liabilities. If accountants were to discontinue the practice of designating which assets and liabilities they believe are current, users could still calculate current and other ratios based on their own concepts of what is current, if disclosure were adequate. The question of which combinations or groupings of assets and liabilities produce ratios with the greatest predictive power is an empirical question. If the attributes of assets and liabilities that are relevant in evaluating solvency were disclosed, there is no reason to expect that accountants could construct ratios with greater predictive power than those that financial statement users could construct.

Calculation Convenience. To a large extent at least, balance sheet classification is a redundant practice. Labeling trade accounts receivable, inventories, and prepaid expenses, for example, as current assets, tells financial statement users nothing about those assets because, with few exceptions, all trade accounts receivable, all inventories, and all prepaid expenses are classified as current.

There is a substantial amount of redundancy in the presentation of all financial statements. If, for example, all of the revenues and expenses of a company are known, presenting the net income figure provides readers with no new information. They could have obtained that figure themselves by merely subtracting the expenses from the revenues. Similarly, the figure labelled total assets on a balance sheet provides no new information if the amounts of all of the individual assets are known.

Redundancy is not necessarily an undesirable attribute of financial statements. Some of it may be quite useful. Presenting an income amount, for example, not only saves the reader time that would otherwise be spent calculating that amount, but it also helps clarify the income statement by directing attention to that amount.

However, the argument that accountants should continue to classify assets and liabilities on the grounds that it is a useful service to financial statement users is not convincing. Although accounting classifications are often used in calculating the current ratio as well as other ratios, accountants should not direct users' attention to the figures generated by a classification system that ignores users' needs.

Many sophisticated financial statement users do not use accounting classifications; they classify assets and liabilities on the basis of their own concepts of what should be called current. Several bankers mentioned this during the interview phase of this study, and Foulke calls attention to it in his book. After pointing out that the definition of current assets in ARB no. 30 begins with the phrase "for accounting purposes" he comments, "This definition as indicated by its first three words is not for credit purposes, management purposes, or analysis purposes; it is solely for 'for accounting purposes.' "[37]

He then lists those assets that he believes should be classified as current and adds, "In this volume, operating supplies and ordinary maintenance material and parts, receivables from officers and employees, no matter how they arose, and prepaid expenses are excluded from current assets."[38]

Summary and Conclusions

ARB no. 30 and current practice based on that bulletin are deficient in many ways. The underlying problem is that the bulletin is based on a fundamental misunderstanding of basic principles of classification and definitions. Although it begins with the statement "The working capital of a borrower has always been of prime interest to grantors of credit," the definitions that follow that opening statement ignore the information needs of credit grantors. Instead of defining current as-

---

37. Roy A. Foulke, *Practical Financial Statement Analysis*, 6th ed. (New York: McGraw-Hill, 1968), p. 71n. See also Morton Backer, *Financial Reporting for Security Investment and Credit Decisions*, NAA Research Studies in Management Reporting no. 3 (New York: National Association of Accountants, 1970), pp. 47-48. Graham, Dodd, and Cottle note, "From the analyst's viewpoint it is best to include in the current assets all cash items that are within the company's control, including those which it does not show as current but *could show* if it so elected" (Benjamin Graham, David L. Dodd, and Sidney Cottle, *Security Analysis: Principles and Technique*, 4th ed. (New York: McGraw-Hill, 1962), p. 203 (emphasis original)).
38. Foulke, *Practical Financial Statement Analysis*, p. 72n.

sets and current liabilities in a way that would provide information useful in evaluating a company's solvency, the committee sought instead to define them in a way that would produce a measure of a company's "true" working capital. Since "true" working capital is a meaningless concept, the result is not surprising. The bulletin has been a failure. Although the lists it contains have provided some uniformity to practice, its definitions are not understandable. Current-noncurrent practices based on the bulletin are described as "inconsistent," "illogical," and "irrational." They not only fail to provide information useful in evaluating solvency; they provide misleading information.

Initially it might seem plausible that the solution to present defective current-noncurrent classification practice is to correct the defect by developing a clearer and more helpful current-noncurrent classification, say a simple one-year dividing line (except that for inventories, for example, it is not simple), but that solution is simplistic. It deals with the symptoms and not the cause of the problem. It is unlikely that financial reporting could be improved by trying to redefine current assets and current liabilities in a way that takes into account users' needs in evaluating solvency. The whole approach by financial statement users to the evaluation of solvency has changed since the practice of classifying assets and liabilities was begun. What might have been a useful practice when it was begun shortly after the turn of the century is unlikely to provide the answers needed by today's users.

There are two basic problems with a simple, dichotomous current-noncurrent classification system as a means of communicating information useful in evaluating a company's solvency. First, two classes are inadequate to disclose the information that needs to be disclosed about some assets and liabilities. Receivables and payables, for example, need to be broken down by maturity dates into more than two classes to provide the information needed to estimate a company's cash receipts and required payments for time periods of several different lengths. Second, the same classification criteria cannot be applied to all assets and liabilities. As a practical matter, inventories, for example, cannot be broken down on the same basis as receivables because of uncertainty as to when they will be sold.

Because of the problems just described, a new approach to providing balance sheet information useful in evaluating a company's solvency is needed. A method of providing information of that type that would replace current-noncurrent classification is described and explained in chapter 5.

5

An Alternative to Current-Noncurrent Classification

The evaluation of Accounting Research Bulletin no. 30 and present current-noncurrent classification practice in chapter 4 led to the conclusion that that approach to providing solvency information does not meet the needs of financial statement users and that it is unlikely to be improved significantly by redefining current assets and current liabilities. This chapter recommends a new approach to reporting solvency information that would replace present classification practice.

Underlying Rationale of Recommended Changes

Three participants in the external financial reporting process can be identified: the accountant, the financial analyst, and the user of external financial data. The primary role of the accountant is to gather financial data, classify it, process it, and present it in the form of general purpose financial statements designed to report the financial position and results of operations of a business enterprise. The internal accountant as a representative of management has initial responsibility for that function, and the external accountant in the role of independent auditor provides assurance concerning the reliability and credibility of the information presented.

The financial analyst analyzes the output of the accountant, that is, the financial statements, and evaluates the company. In doing so he combines information obtained from the financial statements of a company with the information obtained from other sources, and he may take information obtained from financial statements and put it in a form more useful for solving specific problems. Some of the tools used in this process are ratios, pro forma financial statements, and forecasts of future earnings, dividends, and cash receipts and payments. The output of the financial analyst takes the form of recommendations to investors, creditors, and other users of financial data who make decisions based on those recommendations. The role of the financial analyst may, of course, be performed by the user himself rather than a third-party analyst, but analysis is an important function in the overall financial reporting process regardless of who performs it.

The point at which the accountant's responsibility should end and that of the analyst begin is neither clear nor fixed. There is a gray area that lies between preparation and analysis of financial data. Tasks within that area do not fall clearly within the province of either the accountant or the financial analyst. At any given time, society, through its various institutions, assigns responsibility for some of those tasks to accountants while others are left to analysts, but as underlying conditions and attitudes change, responsibilities may be reassigned. There are many examples. Preparation of statements of changes in financial position is now regarded as part of the accounting function, but the forerunners of those statements were considered analytical tools and were prepared by analysts. The same type of shift has also occurred in earnings-per-share data, and accountants are now considering what, if any, responsibility they should assume for forecasts of earnings.

Balance sheet classification of assets and liabilities as current and noncurrent is a practice that lies within the gray area between accounting and financial analysis. The fact that accountants now classify assets and liabilities in balance sheets does not mean that that practice is an inherent part of the accounting process or that it must inevitably continue to be done by accountants.

As pointed out in chapter 2, accountants undertook the classification of assets and liabilities early in this century in response to bankers' needs. Undoubtedly one of the basic reasons that bankers wanted accountants to classify assets and liabilities in balance sheets was that bankers believed that accountants had access to information about the attributes of a company's assets and liabilities that was needed to determine its working capital and that was not otherwise disclosed in its financial statements. Bankers and accountants must

CHAPTER 5: ALTERNATIVE TO CURRENT-NONCURRENT CLASSIFICATION

also have believed that companies either could not or would not disclose that information to outsiders, for if bankers had had access to it, they could have determined the amount of working capital themselves, and the pressure for accountants to undertake that task might never have developed. In essence, current-noncurrent classification developed as a means of partial disclosure; it was a means of disclosing information necessary to determine the amount of a company's working capital without disclosing all of the underlying information needed to decide whether each asset and each liability should be classified as current or noncurrent.

It is understandable how the practice of current-noncurrent classification developed, but the underlying conditions and circumstances that gave rise to that practice have changed. Bankers no longer occupy the dominant position among financial statement users they once did and even they no longer consider adequacy of a company's working capital to be the "alpha and omega" of credit analysis. The whole approach to credit analysis by bankers and others has changed. Credit analysis is now a much broader subject and different types of information are needed. While attention is still devoted to analysis of cash, marketable securities, receivables, inventory, short-term debt, and other items that have traditionally entered into the calculation of working capital, the focus of this attention is different. The analyst is no longer asking whether a company's working capital "cushion" is adequate in the sense that those assets classified as current would be sufficient to pay off those liabilities classified as current, even if some shrinkage in asset values were to occur. Today his analysis of cash, marketable securities, receivables, inventory, and short-term debt, just like his analysis of underground oil reserves, plant and equipment, and long-term debt is directed toward determining (a) whether future cash receipts will be adequate to cover future cash payments and (b) how a company can adapt or adjust to unanticipated cash needs. The significance of ratios that focus on the adequacy of aggregate working capital such as the current ratio, the ratio of working capital to plant and equipment, and the ratio of working capital to long-term debt assume a much less important role in this new approach to credit analysis, while other types of information, such as when receivables and payables are due and how much they are likely to change, assume a much more important role. In summary, the analyst is no longer concerned with whether a receivable is or is not part of working capital; his basic concern now is how much cash will the company receive and when will it be received.

Other conditions have also changed since accountants began the practice of classifying balance sheet items as current and noncurrent. New business practices, new methods of financing, and new methods of accounting have resulted in balance sheet accounts that defy classification as current or noncurrent.

Perhaps one of the most significant changes that has occurred is the change in attitudes toward disclosure of financial information. Financial statement users demand, and companies are willing to disclose, much more detailed information about their financial affairs in supporting schedules and notes to financial statements than at the time accountants began to classify assets and liabilities as current or noncurrent. In today's full disclosure environment, arguments that it would be unreasonable to expect companies to disclose underlying information about the terms and conditions of their assets and liabilities so that bankers and others could classify them as current or noncurrent if they wished to do so would not carry nearly as much weight as they once did. The trend is clearly toward more disclosure of almost any type of information that would be useful to investors, creditors, or other users of financial statements.

The basic philosophy underlying the recommendations made in this study is that accountants should concentrate their attention on disclosing clearly the attributes of assets and liabilities that can be objectively measured and that can reasonably be foreseen to have relevance in estimating a company's future cash receipts and payments and in evaluating its financial flexibility. Exactly how this information should be used, that is, what ratios or other indicators of financial flexibility should be calculated, ought to be left to analysts. Accountants should not bias their data by presenting it in a form most useful for calculation of current or other ratios based on current-noncurrent classification, first because financial statement users have rejected working capital as the center of attention in credit analysis and second because the empirical data available do not support the conclusion that those ratios are the most useful. Which ratio or ratios are the most useful is an empirical question that can be answered by analysts at least as well as by accountants. Furthermore, a priori reasoning suggests that it is unlikely that there is one ratio or even a group of either existing or as yet undeveloped ratios that is most useful for all companies in all industries. More research is needed to determine which ratios or other measures of financial flexibility are the best predictors of financial failure, and accountants can best contribute to this effort by supplying basic information about the attributes of assets and liabilities so that can be done.

Recommendation

The recommended alternative to current-noncurrent classification consists of three parts:

1. Supplemental information about the attributes of specific assets and liabilities should be disclosed.
2. Liabilities should be classified on the basis of different types of sources of credit available to business enterprises.
3. Assets should be arranged on the balance sheet in the conventional order currently in use but should not be classified as current or noncurrent.

Supplemental Information. The principal type of supplemental information needed, in addition to that already disclosed in notes to the financial statements, is information about the amounts and timing of cash receipts and payments from receivables and payables. That information would undoubtedly be useful in estimating a company's cash receipts and required cash payments. A lengthening of the age of a company's receivables, for example, may portend reduced cash receipts the following period.

Disclosing the amounts and timing of receivables and payables cannot be accomplished by simply showing when the balance sheet amounts of those accounts are due. Many receivables and payables are carried at their present values rather than at the amounts of cash to be received or paid in future periods.[1] A company that issues $1 million of ten-year, 10 percent bonds at par, for example, would show a $1 million liability on its balance sheet in spite of the fact that it is obligated to pay a total of $2 million—$100,000 per year for ten years plus an additional $1 million at the end of the tenth year. Similarly, a company that holds a 10 percent note receivable, collectible in ten equal annual installments of $100,000 beginning one year hence, would show a receivable of only $614,457 on its balance sheet in spite of the fact that it expects to receive $1 million from the maker of the note over the next five years. There is no meaningful way of breaking down the $1 million bond liability into the amount that will have to be paid each year because the issuer does not have to pay $1 million; it has to pay $2 million. Similarly, there is no meaningful way of break-

---

1. See AICPA, APB Opinion no. 21, *Interest on Receivables and Payables* (New York: AICPA, 1971).

ing down the $614,457 note receivable into the amount that will be received each year because the holder of the note will not receive $614,457; it will receive $1 million.

Carrying receivables and payables at their present value may be the most useful method of accounting for them for the purpose of measuring the net income of a business enterprise, but it does not provide the most useful information for evaluating a company's solvency.

To evaluate solvency, a person needs to know the gross amounts and timing of cash that will be received or paid, not the present value of those amounts. The balance sheet itself is not, therefore, an appropriate vehicle for disclosing the amounts and timing of future cash receipts and payments that will result from a company's receivables and payables because the totals of those amounts do not equal the present values of the receivables and payables that are shown on its balance sheet. Consequently, the amounts and timing of cash flows from receivables and payables should be disclosed on a separate schedule rather than on the balance sheet. An example of such a schedule is illustrated later in this chapter.

Other information about the attributes of specific assets and liabilities is also useful in estimating the future cash flows of a company and in evaluating its financial flexibility. Much information of this type is now disclosed in the descriptive account titles used on balance sheets and in the notes to the financial statements. Examples include descriptions of the types of inventories held, disclosure of contractual restrictions on the use of various assets such as compensating balance requirements, and disclosure of contingencies related to assets and liabilities. No major recommendations are made in this study for additional disclosures of this type, but several suggestions about specific assets are made later in this chapter.

Classification of Liabilities. Hunt, Williams, and Donaldson distinguish between two basic sources of credit available to a company: spontaneous and negotiated.[2] They describe *spontaneous* or "self generating" sources as those that "grow out of normal patterns of profitable operation without especial effort or conscious decision on the part of owners or managers.[3] Normal trade credit, accrued ex-

---

2. Pearson Hunt, Charles M. Williams, and Gordon Donaldson, *Basic Business Finance*, rev. ed. (Homewood, Ill.: Richard D. Irwin, 1961), pp. 116 and 169.
3. Hunt, Williams, and Donaldson, *Basic Business Finance*, p. 116.

penses, and accrued taxes are examples of that type. *Negotiated sources* are those sources that require conscious effort or specific negotiation on the part of owners or managers to obtain, such as bank loans, sale of commercial paper, sale of bonds, installment purchases, or financing leases.

Although the terms spontaneous and negotiated sources of credit are not widely used, the distinction between those two sources is relevant to the evaluation of both a company's financial flexibility and its forthcoming need for cash.[4] It is relevant to evaluation of financial flexibility because different underlying considerations determine the amount of credit available from each of them. The amount available from spontaneous sources depends on considerations such as the volume of purchases of inventories and supplies, normal credit terms of a company's suppliers, and conventional practices as to frequency of payment of salaries and wages. Credit available from spontaneous sources tends to increase as sales rise and fall as sales decline.

Credit available from negotiated sources, on the other hand, depends more on lenders' evaluations of a company's ability to repay a loan when due. The total amount of credit available to a company through spontaneous sources tends to be limited to a rather narrow range. It is inexpensive or even cost free up to a certain point; beyond that point, it becomes very costly as cash discounts are lost, suppliers refuse to ship goods, and so forth. The amount of credit available from negotiated sources varies widely depending on creditors' evaluations of a company's overall credit worthiness.

The distinction between spontaneous and negotiated sources of credit is also relevant in estimating a company's forthcoming need for cash. Liabilities that arise from spontaneous sources tend to "roll over" more or less automatically; debts that are paid are more or less constantly being replaced by new debts. Consequently, it is not necessary to consider a company's spontaneous liabilities when estimating its forthcoming need for cash unless there is reason to expect that because of a decline in sales or a change in business practices, the amount of those liabilities will change. Negotiated liabilities on the

---

4. R. K. Mautz made a similar distinction in sources of financing. He referred to "primary financing interests" and "incidental financing interests." He argued that incidental financing interests including, for example, trade creditors and employees, "provide financing, but this is neither the primary intent of the particular interest nor the basic reason for the transaction" (R. K. Mautz, *An Accounting Technique for Reporting Financial Transactions*, University of Illinois, Bureau of Economic and Business Research, Special Bulletin no. 7, 1951, pp. 21-22).

other hand, whether short term or long term, are expected to be paid off and they must, therefore, be considered in estimating a company's cash needs. While it is true that some of them may be "rolled over" or refinanced, that is different from the "rolling over" of spontaneous liabilities; it does not occur automatically in the normal course of purchasing goods and paying wages and taxes but requires arm's-length negotiation with a creditor who will once again evaluate the company's overall credit worthiness.

Although most liabilities can be readily identified as arising from either spontaneous or negotiated sources of credit, borderline cases will undoubtedly arise in practice, and it may be necessary to establish arbitrary criteria for deciding how a given liability should be classified. Nevertheless, the distinction is useful and should be used in balance sheet presentations. The distinction is also useful in clarifying and limiting the scope of a new financial statement recommended later in this study, the statement of financing activities.

Arrangement of Assets. The arguments for discontinuing the practice of classifying assets as current or noncurrent were discussed in chapter 4. I know of no basis of asset classification that would increase the usefulness of balance sheets in evaluating solvency and, therefore, recommend none.

The order in which assets are traditionally presented on a balance sheet (cash, marketable securities, trade receivables, inventories, and so forth) has no particular significance, but both accountants and financial statement users are familiar with it.[5] Changing that order would confuse users in much the same way that changing the order of the keys on a typewriter would confuse typists. In the absence of a reason for changing that order, assets should continue to be arranged in the conventional order.

---

5. Trying to list assets in order of liquidity is a waste of time because the term *liquidity* has no agreed-upon operational meaning. Some accountants view liquidity in terms of the number of operational steps an asset must pass through before it is converted into cash (receivables are more liquid than inventory because inventory must be converted into receivables before being converted into cash); some view it in terms of the amount of time that will normally pass before an asset is converted into cash (some inventory will be converted into cash before some receivables); and still others view it in terms of how quickly an asset can be converted into cash (some plant and equipment can be converted into cash faster than some inventory).

Illustration and Discussion of Recommended Presentation

The balance sheet in exhibit 5-1 and the supporting schedule of receivables and financing liabilities in exhibit 5-2 for Example, Inc., illustrate the recommended balance sheet format and the recommended types of additional disclosures.

The basic format of the balance sheet is similar to that now generally used in practice, except that assets and liabilities are not classified as current and noncurrent. The principal differences are the way in which liabilities have been classified and the additional information disclosed in the supporting schedules.

Exhibit 5-1   *Example, Inc.*
BALANCE SHEET

	12/31/77	12/31/76
Assets		
Cash	$ 21,968	$ 15,666
Marketable securities (current market value $23,608 and $29,198)	18,459	21,521
Trade accounts and notes receivable (less allowance for uncollectibles of $973 and $906 respectively)	69,170	65,370
Inventories		
Finished goods	73,610	62,102
Goods in process	22,109	16,998
Raw materials and supplies	13,167	10,605
Total inventories	108,886	189,705
Prepayments	8,164	5,222
Properties:		
Land, buildings, and equipment at cost	349,615	319,101
Accumulated depreciation	(136,171)	(125,591)
Net properties	213,444	193,510
Other assets	1,609	3,873
Total assets	$441,700	$394,867
Liabilities and stockholders' equity		
Operating liabilities (due within one year)		
Trade accounts and notes payable	$ 47,662	$ 49,518
Accrued expenses	29,601	26,401
Total	77,263	75,919
Tax liabilities		
On reported taxable income	13,061	11,996
Withheld from employees and misc.	3,906	4,111
Deferred as a result of timing differences in depreciation	39,664	37,605
Total tax liabilities	56,631	53,712

Liabilities and stockholders' equity (cont.)	12/31/77	12/31/76
Financing liabilities		
Notes payable to banks	$ 48,605	$ 15,513
Mortgage payable	26,000	28,000
7% debentures payable, due 12/31/1995	25,000	25,000
Total financing liabilities	99,605	68,513
Total liabilities	233,499	198,144
Stockholders' equity		
5% convertible preferred stock $100 par value	40,000	70,000
Common stock $10 par value	90,000	70,000
Capital in excess of par	41,609	24,114
Retained earnings	36,592	32,609
Total stockholders' equity	208,201	196,723
Total liabilities and stockholders' equity	$441,700	$394,867

Exhibit 5-2

Example, Inc.
MATURITY SCHEDULE OF RECEIVABLES AND FINANCING LIABILITIES*

	12/31/77	12/31/76
Trade accounts and notes receivable		
Overdue	$ 1,398	$ 1,206
Due within one year	37,111	36,692
Due in 1–2 years	24,906	21,605
Due in 2–3 years	9,205	10,331
Due after 3 years	4,915	4,034
Total	$77,535	$73,868
Financing liabilities		
Due within 1 year	$ 28,435	$ 23,054
Due in 1–2 years	15,670	5,830
Due in 2–3 years	15,510	5,670
Due in 3–4 years	15,350	5,510
Due in 4–5 years	15,190	5,350
Due in 5–10 years	23,550	24,350
Due in 10–15 years	17,710	20,350
Due after 15 years	33,750	33,500
Total	$165,165	$125,614

*Amounts shown represent total cash to be received or paid including both principal and interest. Balance sheet amounts of receivables and financing liabilities are stated at their discounted present values and do not, therefore, equal the amounts shown on this schedule.

Presentation of Assets. For the foregoing reasons, assets are not classified but are arranged in the conventional order.

Receivables. A major recommended change from present practice relates to when receivables are due. That information is included in the maturity schedule of the illustration (exhibit 5-2). Two points are noted about it. First, the total amount to be received does not equal the receivables on the balance sheet because some of the receivables are shown on the balance sheet at their present value. Second, the amount of overdue receivables is identified. Although that amount is rarely, if ever, disclosed in present practice, it would be useful because it would provide an objective indication of the quality of a company's receivables.

Marketable securities. Although current practice requires that investments in marketable securities be classified as current or noncurrent,[6] the basis of that classification is not very clear. ARB no. 43 only states that "marketable securities representing the investment of cash available for current operations" should be classified as current.[7] Many textbook writers interpret that to mean that marketable securities should be classified as current only if it is management's intention to convert them into cash in the near future for normal operating purposes,[8] but the authors of at least one leading textbook state that to be classified as current "there is no requirement that the securities be held for a limited time only or that management express its intent as to the duration of the holding."[9] FASB Statement no. 12 declares that "marketable equity securities owned by an entity shall, in the case of a classified balance sheet, be grouped into separate portfolios according to the current or noncurrent classification of the securities" but provides no guidance about what criteria should be used in making that grouping.

---

6. See AICPA, ARB no. 43, *Restatement and Revision of Accounting Research Bulletins* (New York: AICPA, 1953), chap. 3A. par. 4, and FASB, FASB Statement no. 12, *Accounting for Certain Marketable Securities* (Stamford, Conn.: FASB, 1975), par. 9.
7. ARB no. 43, chap. 3A, par. 4.
8. See, for example, Glenn A. Welsch and Robert N. Anthony, *Fundamentals of Financial Accounting* (Homewood, Ill.: Richard D. Irwin, 1974), p. 262, and Jay M. Smith, Jr. and K. Fred Skousen, *Intermediate Accounting: A Comprehensive Volume*, 6th ed. (Homewood, Ill.: Richard D. Irwin, 1977), p. 132.
9. Walter B. Meigs, A. N. Mosich, Charles E. Johnson, and Thomas F. Keller, *Intermediate Accounting*, 3d ed. (New York: McGraw-Hill, 1974), p. 183.

It seems unlikely that classification of marketable securities into current and noncurrent portfolios provides useful information to financial statement users. Even if the classification is based on management's intent to convert those securities into cash in the near future for normal operating purposes, disclosure of management's intentions would not seem to be useful. Intent is an ephemeral quality that cannot be objectively verified and can be readily changed to meet changing circumstances.

FASB Statement no. 12 prescribes rules for determining income from marketable securities based on whether they are classified as current or noncurrent, but the solution to that problem is to amend the statement rather than retain the distinction for the purpose of implementing those rules. Income measurement is not improved by basing it on "inconsistent," "illogical," and "irrational" classification rules.

The amount of marketable securities held is likely to be important information in the evaluation of a company's financial flexibility. The relevant attributes of marketable securities for that purpose are (1) whether the securities held are readily marketable, (2) how much they can be sold for, and (3) whether their sale or the use of the proceeds of sale are restricted.

That information can be readily disclosed by carefully defining what is meant by the term marketable securities, by disclosing the market values of those securities, and by disclosing any restrictions on their sale or use.[10] If that information is disclosed, no purpose is served in classifying marketable securities as current or noncurrent.

Inventories. Nearly all inventories are classified as current, but a few companies classify a portion of them as noncurrent on the

---

10. The definition of marketable equity securities in par. 7 of FASB Statement no. 12 would probably be appropriate for this purpose. That statement defines them as follows: "*Marketable*, as applied to an equity security, means an equity security as to which sales prices or bid and asked prices are currently available on a national securities exchange (i.e., those registered with the Securities and Exchange Commission) or in the over-the-counter market. In the over-the-counter market, an equity security shall be considered marketable when a quotation is publicly reported by the National Association of Securities Dealers Automatic Quotations System or by the National Quotations Bureau, Inc. (provided, in the latter case, that quotations are available from at least three dealers). Equity securities traded in foreign markets shall be considered marketable when such markets are of a breadth and scope comparable to those referred to above. Restricted stock does not meet this definition."

grounds that they are slow moving or in excess of normal requirements. Mobil, for example, included this note in its description of major accounting policies in its 1973 annual report:

> In certain foreign countries, Mobil is required to maintain crude oil and products inventories at levels specified by government authorities, considered to be greater than normal working requirements. Effective January 1, 1973, the portion of the inventories considered to be greater than normal working requirements is included on the balance sheet under Investments and Long Term Receivables and is not revalued when changes occur in average cost.

That type of information is undoubtedly useful in evaluating a company's financial flexibility but it is not necessary to classify inventories as current or noncurrent to accomplish it. The important point is that disclosure be made of amounts held in excess of normal requirements, not that the excess be labeled as current or noncurrent.

Presentation of Liabilities. Three basic types of liabilites are identified on the Example, Inc., balance sheet: operating, tax, and financing. Operating and tax liabilities arise out of spontaneous sources of credit; financing liabilities arise out of negotiated sources. The term "financing liabilities" is used rather than "negotiated liabilities" simply because it is more likely to be readily understood.

The basic rationale for breaking down a company's liabilities into three categories, as previously explained, is that different underlying considerations determine the level of each type. A person concerned with estimating a company's future need for cash is more concerned with expected *changes* in the level of its liabilities than with the absolute level of its liabilities, because only changes in liabilities are relevant when estimating a company's future cash receipts and payments. Classifying liabilities on the basis of the underlying considerations that determine the level of each category should, therefore, provide useful insight into a company's need for cash to extinguish liabilities. Also, the financial significance of changes that have occurred in a company's liabilities during the past year can probably be more readily grasped if its total liabilities are broken down into the three relatively homogeneous groups suggested.

All of the operating liabilities of Example, Inc., are due within one year, but some companies, of course, have operating liabilities (deferred revenue, for example) that are not due for several years. If amounts applicable to future years are material, they should be disclosed. Simple disclosure of the total amount applicable to future years would usually be adequate, but if the amounts applicable to each of several future years are large, the amount applicable to each year should be disclosed.

Three types of tax liabilities can be identified on the basis of their effects on the future cash flows of an enterprise: (1) those due currently, including corporate income taxes, taxes withheld from employees, real estate taxes, sales taxes, and so forth; (2) income taxes deferred as a result of timing differences in the recognition of revenue or expense for tax and financial reporting purposes; and (3) deferred investment tax credits. Since different underlying factors cause each of these three basic types to change, each should be disclosed separately. The first type tends to be relatively small, and, although it fluctuates during the year, it tends to be relatively stable from year to year. The second type, deferred income taxes, fluctuates as a result of timing differences in the recognition of revenue and expense for tax and financial reporting purposes. A person interested in estimating the future cash needs of a company is, of course, interested in when deferred tax credits will reverse because the effective tax rate will then increase. When that reversal will take place cannot be stated directly, but an awareness of the nature of the timing difference that gave rise to tax deferrals, such as differences in depreciation, use of the installment method of recognizing revenue for tax purposes, and so forth, is useful in providing financial statement users with some insight into the events that will cause deferred taxes to reverse and that information should, therefore, be disclosed. The third type of tax liability, deferred investment tax credits, will not, of course, require a future outlay of cash. A statement of how deferred investment tax credits will be amortized would be useful in estimating future reported income, but that amortization will not affect a company's future cash payments.

As noted above, operating liabilities and tax liabilities result from and are incidental to the normal operations of a company, whereas financing liabilities result from specific negotiations between management and the suppliers of funds. Disclosure of the amounts, the nature of changes in, and the terms of, financing liabilities is likely to provide financial statement users with important insights into a company's financial policies, and those liabilities are, therefore, likely to be of primary interest to users. Consequently, it is of particular importance that financing liabilities be described fully.

Three basic types of information about the financing liabilities of Example, Inc., are described in the illustrative statements: (1) the type of liability (notes payable to banks, mortgage payable, and debentures payable), (2) the book value of each of those liabilities, (that is, the present value at the time the liability was incurred plus or minus adjustments since that date), and (3) the amount of cash that will have to be paid under the terms of all financing liabilities for each of the next five years, for each of the two succeeding five-year periods, and in total for all subsequent years.

Trend to More Disclosure. For many years, there has been a clear trend toward disclosing more information about the attributes of specific assets and liabilities in the notes to the financial statements. Much of that information is clearly relevant in evaluating a company's financial flexibility and estimating its future cash receipts and payments. Disclosure of credit commitments, compensating balance requirements, and minimum amounts due under long-term leases are clear examples. New issues will undoubtedly arise in the future. When they do, the guiding consideration should be whether the proposed disclosure can reasonably be expected to be useful in evaluating a company's financial flexibility and estimating its future cash receipts and payments.

Summary and Implications of Recommendations

The basic recommendation made in this chapter is that additional information about the attributes of individual assets and liabilities be disclosed as an alternative to classifying assets and liabilities as current or noncurrent. An example was presented to illustrate the type of additional information that should be disclosed and suggestions were made concerning how that disclosure could be accomplished. The recommendations made are modest; they would not require a radical departure from present disclosure practices nor would they be costly to implement. The principal change recommended is in the disclosures relating to receivables and payables.

The rationale underlying the recommendations made in this chapter is that they would provide more useful information for evaluating a company's solvency than present practice based on current-noncurrent classification. Present practice is directed toward calculation of the current ratio and other measures based on the concept of working capital as a measure of solvency; the alternative proposal emphasizes the disclosure of additional data that can be combined and used in various ways, although the data are directed to the solvency dimension of financial statement analysis.

It is impossible to foresee exactly how the additional information recommended will be used. The current ratio has been used so widely and for so long that in spite of empirical evidence that it has only mediocre predictive power compared to other ratios, some form of it will no doubt continue to be used. That, however, could still be done under the alternative recommended; the basic information needed to calculate that ratio would still be available. But if accountants cease to orient disclosure toward the calculation of the current ratio and other ratios designed to measure adequacy of working capital, other measures will no doubt be developed.

Perhaps the ratio of cash, marketable securities, trade receivables, and inventories to operating liabilities plus tax liabilities (possibly excluding deferred taxes) or the ratio of cash, marketable securities, and trade receivables to financing liabilities due within one year would have greater power to predict financial failure than the present current ratio. The point is that there are many different types of ratios that could be calculated if more generalized data were presented, that the predictive power of ratios is an empirical matter that can be measured statistically, and that there is no reason to assume, as accountants have implicitly done for years, that the current and other ratios that measure adequacy of working capital are the ones that should be used in solvency evaluation. Accountants are likely to serve society best by presenting general information that can be used in different ways. The task of deciding how that information should be used, whether in ratios, in forecasts of future cash flows, or in as yet undeveloped measures of financial flexibility, should be left to those whose task it is to analyze and interpret accounting data.

6

Funds Statements: Underlying Issues

Two principal ways in which a company reports solvency related information are identified in chapter 1: classification of its assets and liabilities as current and noncurrent and presentation of a statement of changes in financial position. Chapters 3, 4, and 5 discuss present classification practice and recommended changes. This chapter and chapter 7 discuss statements of changes in financial position. The historical development of those statements is traced, and present practice in presenting them is evaluated; other statements that would better achieve the objectives of those statements are recommended, illustrated, and discussed in chapter 7.

Statements of changes in financial position were known as funds statements for many years. Both the old as well as the new titles are objectionable for reasons discussed later, but the name "funds statement" is used in the discussion that follows because it is less cumbersome than "statements of changes in financial position."

Historical Development of Funds Statements

Although earlier examples of funds statements appeared both in practice[1] and on CPA exams,[2] the first extended discussion of them is

---

1. Several examples are reproduced in Lawrence S. Rosen, *A Critical Examination of "Funds" Statement Concepts*, unpublished doctoral dissertation, University of Washington, 1966, pp. 269-280. See also discussion, pp. 11-19.
2. Rosen, *Examination of "Funds,"* pp. 17-18 and L.S. Rosen and Don T. DeCoster, " 'Funds' Statements: A Historical Perspective," *Accounting Review*, 44 (January, 1969): 126.

87

found in the 1908 edition of William Morse Cole's once-popular textbook, *Accounts: Their Construction and Interpretation*. According to Rosen, "Cole probably was influential in popularizing one particular form of statement which remained in the accounting literature for about a generation."[3]

Where Got-Where Gone Statements. The statement popularized by Cole was simply a statement of changes in all balance sheet accounts displayed in two columns: one labeled "where got" for credit changes and the other labeled "where gone" for debit changes. Cole's discussion of "where got-where gone" statements appeared as part of a chapter on interpretation of balance sheets because he saw them as an analytical tool for analyzing solvency changes as reflected on a company's beginning and ending balance sheets, not as a means of reporting information that differed from or supplemented that already found on a company's balance sheet. He argued—

> It is obvious that an important result of constructing such a table . . . is the possibility of seeing from it at a glance the changes in solvency. Certain kinds of assets are always good, certain kinds are sometimes bad, and a few kinds are usually bad. Certain kinds of liability are not suspicious, and certain kinds are often so.[4]

Statement of Changes in Working Capital. Statements of changes in working capital were introduced during the 1920s. Funds statements of that type gained widespread attention in accounting literature largely as the result of the efforts of H.A. Finney, author of leading accounting textbooks and former editor of the "Students' Department" of the *Journal of Accountancy*. Both of those positions enabled Finney to exert considerable influence over accounting issues.[5]

During the early 1920s, funds statement problems appeared frequently on CPA examinations. At that time unofficial solutions and comments on those solutions were published in the "Students' De-

---

3. Rosen, *Examination of "Funds,"* p. 11.
4. William Morse Cole, *Accounts: Their Construction and Interpretation*, rev. and enl. ed. (Boston: Houghton Mifflin, 1915), p. 132.
5. During the 1920s leading accounting textbooks and the views of the editor of the "Students' Department" were important sources of support of accounting principles. The SEC was not formed until 1934, and the committee on accounting procedure was not organized until 1938.

CHAPTER 6: FUNDS STATEMENTS

partment" of the *Journal*.[6] After reviewing Finney's comments on CPA examination funds statement problems and solutions, Rosen and DeCoster observed as follows:

> Regardless of whether the question requested "a short statement showing the funds realized during the year and disposition made thereof" or vaguely asked for a statement for a banker, Finney employed a report format which showed the causes of a change in working capital.[7]

From this and a review of his other writings, they concluded that—

> Through *frequent* repetition of his views, Finney, more than anyone else seems to have turned the "academic tide" at that time in favor of the liquidity concept—in particular, working capital.[8]

Finney's rationale for emphasizing working capital is not stated explicitly in his writings, but it can be inferred. He was particularly concerned with working capital measurement and analysis in general and the importance of working capital in bank credit analysis in particular. He devoted more space in his textbook to discussion of working capital than the authors of other accounting textbooks did at the time.[9] He undoubtedly agreed with A.C. Littleton's argument:

> The ability to pay current debts depends more on the *flow* of working capital than upon the *size* of the working capital investment . . . and therefore measures of flow are more important in analyzing financial condition than is the current ratio.[10]

The results of the frequent appearance of funds statement problems on CPA examinations during the 1920s and Finney's extensive discussion of the topic in the *Journal of Accountancy* were, not surpri-

---

6. See the *Journal of Accountancy*, 29 (March, 1920): 228-231; 32 (July, 1921): 64-67; 34 (August, 1922): 142-145; 34 (December, 1922): 406-407; 35 (January, 1923): 53-55; 36 (December, 1923): 460-472; 37 (April, 1924): 304-308; 38 (July, 1924): 58-62; 39 (May, 1925): 424-430; 39 (June, 1925): 497-511; 40 (October, 1925): 305-313; 40 (December, 1925): 464-469; and 41 (March, 1926): 215-229.
7. Rosen and DeCoster, " 'Funds' Statements," p.129.
8. Rosen and DeCoster, " 'Funds' Statements," p.128 (emphasis original).
9. The 1934 edition of his intermediate textbook, *Principles of Accounting—Intermediate*, contains three full chapters on the subject of working capital.
10. A. C. Littleton, "The 2 to 1 Ratio Analyzed," *Certified Public Accountant*, 6, no. 8 (August, 1926): 246 (emphasis original).

singly, that funds statements soon came to be widely discussed in accounting textbooks, and textbook writers adopted the working capital concept of funds as the "proper" one to use. With few exceptions, that approach went unchallenged until the 1950s. Hector R. Anton observed as late as 1962 that textbook writers supported the working capital concept of funds "almost unanimously."[11]

Alternatives to Changes in Working Capital. Funds statements were a favorite topic of debate in accounting literature during the 1950s and 1960s, and the concept of funds to be used in preparing them was the most controversial aspect of that debate. Among the many diverse views presented during that period, two recurring themes can be readily identified. Some writers either implicitly or explicitly accepted Finney's view that the purpose of the funds statement is to show changes in the solvency of a firm as measured by some "pool" of "liquid" resources, but they argued that working capital is too broad a "pool"—it takes into account assets that are too far removed from cash. They advocated a narrower concept of funds. Maurice Moonitz, for example, advocated a "net money assets available for disposition" concept, which he defined as "the sum of cash on hand and in banks, marketable securities held as secondary cash reserves, and current receivables, less the current liabilities that will be paid by quick assets in the near future."[12] Hector R. Anton advocated a concept of "money resources," which was even narrower; it included only "cash or promises held to receive cash . . . that are available for disposition as needed in the normal course of business."[13]

Other writers, however, saw the funds statement in an entirely different way. They denied the existence of a "pool" of "liquid" re-

---

11. Hector R. Anton, *Accounting for the Flow of Funds* (New York: Houghton Mifflin, 1962), p.83. See also Donald A. Corbin, "Proposals for Improving Funds Statements," *Accounting Review*, 36 (July, 1961): 398.
12. Maurice Moonitz, "Reporting on the Flow of Funds," *Accounting Review*, 31 (July, 1956): 379.
13. Anton, *Accounting for the Flow of Funds*, p.37. It is surprising that the argument over the definition of funds did not spill over into the definition of current assets. If one believes that inventories, for example, are too far removed from cash to be included in the concept of funds used in preparing a funds statement, it would seem logical to argue that inventories also should be excluded from current assets so that the "pool" of "liquid" resources shown on the balance sheet would tie in with the "pool" used as the basis of preparing the funds statement. That argument, however, could not be found in the literature.

sources that serves as a measure of solvency and whose changes need to be explained. They saw the funds statement as a device for explaining changes in *all* balance sheet accounts. Louis Goldberg is one of the principal advocates of this point of view:

> If funds are regarded as cash or working capital or current assets, a pool available in some quantity at any given point of time is strongly and perhaps inevitably suggested. But the fact that *all* funds derived during a period have been applied *somehow* during the period suggests that there is never any pool of funds, but rather that the processes of derivation and application are simultaneous. From this point of view the balance sheet becomes a by-product not only of the process of matching revenue and changes, but also of the flow of resources; at one and the same time it is integrally related to the revenue statement and the funds statement, which are the representation of those dynamic processes. Thus, while the revenue statement is a financial summary of the activities of an enterprise over a period . . . , the funds statement is likewise a financial summary of the same activities, but by emphasizing changes in balance sheet items it exhibits these activities in a different light and makes it possible to express the balance sheet items in a dynamic rather than a static sense.[14]

Goldberg distinguished between (1) fund events that he identified as "external transactions" or "dealings between an undertaking and other persons" and (2) nonfund events that he identified as "internal operations" or "happenings within the undertaking not affecting relations with other persons."[15] He agreed with Cole's concept of funds as "resources" or "values" because Cole's concept was "more cogent, more satisfying and more rational" than the working capital concept,[16] but he also defined funds himself as "a notional concept equivalent to the *flow* of resources which is expressed in the transaction of a notional accounting entity with other entities."[17]

Donald A. Corbin, another leading advocate of a broad concept of funds, shared Goldberg's views. After noting that Goldberg had taken "the reasonable position that it is necessary to have a concept of funds which will prove satisfying *in all cases*,"[18] Corbin defined funds as "assets or resources, i.e. as all purchasing power" and added that

---

14. Louis Goldberg, "The Funds Statement Reconsidered," *Accounting Review*, 26 (October, 1951): 489-490 (emphasis original).
15. Goldberg, "Funds Statement Reconsidered," pp. 487-488.
16. Goldberg, "Funds Statement Reconsidered," p.485.
17. Goldberg, "Funds Statement Reconsidered," p.489.
18. Donald A. Corbin, "Proposals for Improving Funds Statements," *Accounting Review*, 36 (July, 1961): 399 (emphasis original).

Only one basic question regarding any net change revealed by comparative balance sheets need be asked under the proposed definition of funds as resources and the rule of showing only external physical flow of assets: "Was there a physical flow of assets into or out of the business entity in connection with the balance sheet change?" If the answer is yes, a source or application of funds should be shown in the funds statement; if no, the change should be eliminated.[19]

Corbin did not have in mind a mere expansion of the conventional funds statement to include a few transactions that did not actually affect working capital but might be construed as if they had, such as the acquisition of plant and equipment in exchange for securities. He specifically rejected the idea that working capital has anything to do with a funds statement. The example he presented included sources and uses of funds such as changes in inventories, current receivables, and payables and contained no mention of working capital.[20]

As author of Accounting Research Study no. 2, published by the AICPA in 1961, Perry Mason undertook to provide guidance to the Accounting Principles Board on how to resolve the controversy over the funds concept to use in preparing a funds statement. Mason discussed several concepts of funds and appeared to agree with Goldberg and Corbin. He cited their works with approval and stated that funds should be defined as "purchasing or spending power, or as all financial resources, arising . . . from external rather than internal transactions," a definition clearly consistent with the concepts they advocated.[21] He illustrated that concept, however, with a statement that was basically a statement of changes in working capital that showed the acquisition of plant in exchange for common stock as if it had been both a source and use of working capital.[22] That clearly was not what Goldberg and Corbin had in mind, as Corbin later pointed out.[23]

Authoritative Pronouncements on Funds Statements. In October, 1963, the Accounting Principles Board issued APB Opinion no.

---

19. Corbin, "Improving Funds Statements," p.402.
20. Corbin, "Improving Funds Statements," p.404.
21. Perry Mason, *"Cash Flow" Analysis and the Funds Statement*, AICPA Accounting Research Study no. 2 (New York: AICPA, 1961), p. 54. See also p. 90.
22. Mason, *"Cash Flow" Analysis*, p.55.
23. Donald A. Corbin and Russell Taussig, "The AICPA Funds Statement Study," *Journal of Accountancy*, 114 (July, 1962): 57-62.

CHAPTER 6: FUNDS STATEMENTS

3, the first official pronouncement on the subject of funds statements. The opinion recommended, among other things, that funds statements be included in financial reports as "supplementary information" and that when preparing a funds statement for presentation in annual reports, "a concept broader than that of working capital . . . be used which can be characterized or defined as 'all financial resources'."

Although APB Opinion no. 3 was hailed by the *Journal of Accountancy* as a "major step" that had "considerable impact,"[24] it did little to resolve the controversy raging in accounting literature over what was meant by the term "funds" in a funds statement. The working capital concept of funds was deeply embedded in the thought processes of a whole generation of accountants, and, in practice, most companies continued to tie their funds statements to changes in working capital. The enigmatic "all financial resources" definition of funds recommended in Opinion no. 3 was interpreted to mean that certain kinds of transactions, principally the acquisition of plant and equipment in exchange for debt or equity securities, should be shown on a funds statement as if they had affected working capital even though they did not.[25]

APB Opinion no. 19, the second major pronouncement of funds statements, issued in 1971, changed the title of the funds statement to the "statement of changes in financial position" (the statement) and required that it be presented as a basic financial statement when financial statements purporting to present financial position and results of operations are issued. That opinion requires that the statement prominently disclose working capital or cash provided from or used in operations for the period, and if the working capital format is used, it requires a supporting schedule of net changes in each element of working capital. It also prescribes the content of the statement in some detail. Specific disclosures required are as follows:

---

24. "Not to Mislead the Public," editorial in *Journal of Accountancy*, 118 (July, 1964): 23-24.

25. The AICPA Accounting Principles Board had apparently received indications that the meaning of the "all financial resources" concept of funds was unclear after Mason had recommended it in his research study. In summarizing comments received on that study, the research staff of the AICPA observed, "It was expected that some teachers would object to this departure from conventional textbook practice, but some practitioners also found it unacceptable, usually because of its lack of preciseness" ("Comments on 'Cash Flow' Analysis and the Funds Statement," *Journal of Accountancy*, 114 (September, 1962): 65).

a. Outlays for purchase of long-term assets . . . .
  b. Proceeds from sale . . . of long-term assets not in the normal course of business, less related expenses involving the current use of working capital or cash.
  c. Conversion of long-term debt or preferred stock to common stock.
  d. Issuance, assumption, redemption, and repayment of long-term debt.
  e. Issuance, redemption, or purchase of capital stock for cash or for assets other than cash.
  f. Dividends in cash or in kind or other distributions to shareholders (except stock dividends and stock split-ups. . .).

Opinion no. 19 probably improved financial reporting; statements of changes in financial position are now included in the financial reports of all companies, their form is substantially more uniform, and they contain more information than before the opinion was issued.[26] But like Opinion no. 3, Opinion no. 19 did little, if anything, to clarify the underlying concept of funds to be used as the basis of preparing those statements. The APB scrupulously avoided all reference to the "all financial resources" concept of funds recommended in Opinion no. 3. Instead, it concluded that "the statement . . . should be based on a broad concept embracing all changes in financial position" and noted that "in view of the broadened concept of the Funds Statement adopted, . . . the title of the statement [should] be changed to 'Statement of Changes in Financial Position'." The concept was not explained, however, and the reader was left to ponder whether it was something even broader than the "all financial resources" concept that the board had recommended eight years earlier in Opinion no. 3. Underlying the board's decision to change the name of the statement from a funds statement to a statement of changes in financial position and to avoid any mention of the word "funds" in its recommendation may have been a belief that the problem of how to

---

26. Although paragraph 9 of the opinion provides that "each entity should adopt the presentation that is most informative in its circumstances" and paragraph 11 states that "provided that these guides are met, the statement may take whatever form gives the most useful portrayal of the financing and investing activities and the changes in financial position of the reporting entity," the disclosure requirements of the opinion have the effect of circumscribing considerably the form of the statement.

define funds would simply go away. Unfortunately it has not. The controversy continues unabated in accounting literature.[27]

Although companies now use the recommended title, "statement of changes in financial position," most such statements are still "tied" to working capital in the sense that the change in working capital balances the sources and uses of funds.[28] The amount of working capital or cash provided by operations is now added to the fair value of stock exchanged for plant and equipment and the book value of stock exchanged for convertible securities, transactions that have nothing to do with working capital, cash or any other reasonable interpretation of the word "funds," and the total is then typically labelled "funds provided" or "total sources of funds."[29] The financial statement user as well as the accountant, himself, are then left to wonder what this elusive, enigmatic, and confusing thing called "funds" really is![30]

---

27. See, for example, Stephen L. Buzby and Haim Falk, "A New Approach to the Funds Statement," *Journal of Accountancy*, 137 (January, 1974): 55-61; Aubrey C. Roberts and David R. L. Gabhart, "Statement of Funds: A Glimpse of the Future," *Journal of Accountancy*, 133 (April, 1972): 54-59; and J. W. Giese and T. P. Klammer, "Achieving the Objectives of APB Opinion no. 19," *Journal of Accountancy*, 137 (March, 1974): 54-61.
28. Spiller and Virgil found that 131 of the 143 publicly held companies studied by them employed the working capital concept of funds (Earl A. Spiller and Robert L. Virgil, "Effectiveness of APB Opinion no. 19 in Improving Funds Reporting," *Journal of Accounting Research*, 12 (Spring, 1974): 115). See also Hortense Goodman and Leonard Lorensen, *Illustrations of the Statement of Changes in Financial Position*, (New York: AICPA, 1974), p. 3 and Giese and Klammer, "Achieving the Objectives of APB Opinion no. 19," p. 57.
29. It is ironic that although businessmen typically think of short-term bank borrowing and the sale of marketable securities as sources of funds, neither of these transactions appears on a funds statement as it is now prepared. The conversion of convertible debt into common stock, on the other hand, is usually considered a nonfund or a "paper" transaction, but it does appear on a funds statement!
30. Spiller and Virgil comment that "although the opinion often embraces a concept of funds broader than working capital, it does not explicitly call for a change in concept. Rather, the focus is on disclosure. As long as certain types of transactions are disclosed in the required way, apparently any, all, or no underlying concept of funds is appropriate" (Spiller and Virgil, "Improving Funds Reporting," p. 115).

Role of Funds Statements in Financial Reporting

The meaning of the term "funds" needs to be clarified but it is not the most fundamental issue; it is merely a symptom of the confusion that exists over the role of the funds statement in the overall financial reporting process. There is substantial agreement among both accountants and users of financial statements that while both the conventional balance sheet and income statement are useful, they are not adequate to report all of the information that needs to be reported and that some type of "third" financial statement, whatever it might be called, is needed to fill important gaps in the financial reporting process. There is little agreement, however, on exactly what those gaps are and on the form that third statement should take. The lack of agreement stems in part from legitimate differences of opinion over users' needs. It is also due in part, however, to widespread misunderstanding of two basic issues: (1) the relationship between the activities of a business enterprise and how those activities, particularly the profit directed activities, affect its financial position and (2) inherent limitations of financial statements as a means of communicating economic data. That misunderstanding is the cause of much of the confusion that exists over both the role of the funds statement in the overall financial reporting process and the controversy over the definition of funds.

Business Activities and Financial Statements. The activities of business enterprises may be classified as operating, financing, and investing. Operating activities are those activities directly related to the purchase and sale of raw materials, supplies, and merchandise, the conversion of raw material and supplies into finished goods and services, the sale of finished goods and services, and the servicing of goods and services sold previously. Financing activities are those activities directly related to obtaining capital including, for example, the borrowing and repayment of debt, the issuance and reaquisition of a company's stock, the conversion of securities into common stock, and the payment of dividends. Investment activities include the purchase and sale of securities of various types (excluding a company's own securities) and the purchase and sale of plant and equipment that is used in the production, distribution, and maintenance of other goods and services. The lines between those different types of activities are not clear, but the distinction is, nevertheless, useful for this discussion.

Each of the activities identified affects the financial position of a company in many ways. Some affect its net assets; others do not.

Some affect its cash position; others do not. Some affect its inventories; others do not, and so forth. Moreover, each activity simultaneously affects many different aspects of a company's financial position. A cash sale, for example, affects its cash, inventories, monetary assets, nonmonetary assets, assets classified as current, total assets, owners' equity, and retained earnings.

Financial statements are the means by which the results of business activities are reported to persons interested in those activities. They are, in essence, maps of economic territory. They are of two basic types: position statements and flow statements. Position statements portray various aspects of a company's financial position; flow statements portray the effects of a company's business activities on some aspect or aspects of its financial position.

Since the financial position of a company has many different aspects, it follows that many different types of flow statements could be prepared. Statements that show the effect of business activities on cash, on total assets, on long-term liabilities, or on fixed assets are all examples of flow financial statements.

In practice, a single type of flow statement, the income statement, dominates financial reporting. As noted in chapter 1, for many years accounting theorists as well as groups responsible for promulgating accounting standards have been concerned with income measurement-valuation issues almost exclusively.[31]

Income statements are often described as the "connecting link" between successive balance sheets, but that is, at best, a half-truth. An income statement does not report all of the activities that caused the balance sheet to change; it reports only the effects of selected operating activities,[32] selected financing activities (for example, repayment of debt at less than book value), and selected investment activities (for example, sale of plant at more or less than book value)

---

31. Maurice Moonitz pointed out in the preface to Mason's study that accounting has "identified itself with the measurement of corporate net profit, to the virtual exclusion of other aspects of business activity" (Perry Mason, "*Cash Flow" Analysis*, pp. xi-xii). Robert K. Jaedicke and Robert T. Sprouse noted similarly that "the statement of income (flow) has traditionally been emphasized almost to the exclusion of other useful flows" (Robert K. Jaedicke and Robert T. Sprouse, *Accounting Flows: Income, Funds, and Cash* (Englewood Cliffs, N.J.: Prentice-Hall, 1965), p. 6).
32. Many operating activities including, for example, the purchase of merchandise, collection of receivables, and payment for operating supplies are not reported on its income statement.

on the net assets of a company. It does not report the effects of even those activities on other aspects of a company's financial position, such as its cash position, its inventory position, or its total assets. It does not even report the effect on net assets of all activities that affect the net assets of a company; it shows only the effect of those activities included in the measurement of net income. Other activities that affect net assets are shown on other flow statements, that is, the statement of retained earnings and the statement of other changes in owner's equity.

The dominance of the income statement and its description as *the* statement of operations has had profound effects on attitudes toward financial reporting in general and on funds statements in particular. Some of the effects are discussed below, but first it is necessary to comment briefly on certain limitations inherent in financial statements.

Limitations of Financial Statements. A business enterprise engages in a myriad of activities each period, and each of those activities affects its financial position in many different ways. No geographic map could portray clearly changes in annual rainfall, changes in educational level of the population, changes in agricultural crops, and changes in unemployment in a given geographic area; different maps are needed to portray changes in each characteristic or limited combination of characteristics of the territory. Similarly, no financial statement can portray clearly the effects on all aspects of a company's financial position of all of the activities it engaged in during the year. To design a financial statement that communicates clearly, it is necessary to decide which activities are the objects of attention (for example, operating, financing, investing, all of these, or some of these) and second, which of the various aspects of financial position that those activities affect should be portrayed (for example, the effect on working capital, the effect on net monetary assets, the effect on net assets, and so forth). The number of different types of flow statements that could be prepared is almost limitless; which ones companies should present should be based on their perceived usefulness.

Unrealistic and Worthless Objectives. The widespread misunderstanding of the effects of business activities on a company's financial position and the nature and role of financial statements, particularly the income statement, has resulted in setting up unrealistic and worthless objectives for funds statements. Attempts to design statements to achieve those objectives have led to frustration and confusion and have retarded the development of more meaningful and readily understood statements.

Many accountants view the funds statements as a statement that is supposed to interpret and explain or provide backup details for the "basic" information found in the balance sheet and income statement rather than report a different type of information useful for a different purpose. Nearly all authors of accounting textbooks at least imply that objective by placing their discussion of funds statements near the end of the book either immediately before, as part of, or immediately following, the chapter on analysis of financial statements. Some of them also state it explicitly. For example:

> Basically, the funds flow statement provides the same information provided by the balance sheet and income statement, but with a different emphasis.[33]

> Information on this less formal report is intended to provide a more detailed understanding of the firm than does information on the more structured balance sheet and income statement.[34]

> The [funds statement] has as its central purpose the explanation of the causes of the changes in assets, liabilities, and owners' equity that occurred during the period.[35]

At least one author views the presentation of a funds statement as a way of making the other statements more readable:

> The funds statement is intended to make financial statements easier to read. For example, there are fewer lines of information. . . . The language is lighter and more informal. The dollar amounts are invariably smaller and easier to grasp. The presence of the funds statement generally makes the reading of financial statements more inviting.[36]

There are probably at least three reasons for the belief that the purpose of the funds statement is to interpret and explain the information in the "basic" financial statements. One stems from the fact

---
33. John Dearden and John Shank, *Financial Accounting and Reporting* (Englewood Cliffs, N.J.: Prentice-Hall, 1975), p. 49.
34. I. Eugene McNeill, *Financial Accounting: A Decision Information System*, 2d ed. (Pacific Palisades, Calif.: Goodyear Publishing Co., 1974), pp. 421-422.
35. Glenn A. Welsch and Robert N. Anthony, *Fundamentals of Financial Accounting*, rev. ed. (Homewood, Ill.: Richard D. Irwin, 1977), p. 589.
36. David H. Li, *Accounting for Management Analysis* (Columbus, Ohio: Charles E. Merrill Books, Inc., 1964), p. 147.

noted earlier that the forerunners of present-day funds statements were simply statements of changes in balance sheet accounts; they were analytical tools rather than financial statements, and they contained no information that was not also shown in the balance sheet. Although that is no longer true of present-day funds statements, the belief continues. It was no doubt reinforced by the writings of Goldberg, Corbin, and others who viewed funds statements as devices for explaining changes in all balance sheet accounts resulting from "external transactions" and who defined funds vaguely as "assets," "values," "all purchasing power," or "all financial resources."

A second reason for the belief that funds statements are meant to interpret and explain the information on the "basic" financial statements stems from the way in which funds statements are prepared. Accounting records are designed to facilitate preparation of the income statement, not the funds statement. The information needed to prepare the income statement is collected in a group of nominal accounts called revenue and expense accounts. In a similar manner, another group of nominal accounts could be set up to collect the information needed to prepare a funds statement, but that step has never been taken. The information needed to prepare a funds statement is typically collected on a work sheet and is never recorded in the accounts. Changes in a company's balance sheet accounts are adjusted on the work sheet using information obtained from its income statement together with information obtained directly from its internal records. That process of collecting the information used in preparing the funds statement has undoubtedly contributed to the belief that the purpose of a funds statement is to explain the "basic" information in the balance sheet and income statement rather than to report a different type of information that is useful in its own right.

A third, and perhaps the most important, reason for the belief that funds statements are meant to interpret and explain the information in the "basic" financial statements is that many accountants do not think in terms of any effect of operations other than the income effect because of the widespread misconception that an income statement is *the* statement of operations. Their preoccupation with income measurement and reporting issues, in other words, has blinded them to the potential for reporting other effects of operations that would be useful in solvency analysis.

Another widespread belief about the role of funds statements is that they are somehow supposed to show what "happened" to a company's profits or where its profits "went."[37] The common, yet confusing, practice of showing net income as a source of funds, adjusting it for "nonfund" items such as depreciation, amortization, and changes in long-term deferred income taxes payable to determine funds provided by operations can undoubtedly be attributed, at least in part, to that belief. If one believes that funds statements are supposed to show what "happened" to a company's profit, then it seems reasonable to show profit as a source of funds—yet once profit is shown as a source of funds, to make the funds statement balance, it is necessary to show depreciation and other nonfund items as if they affected funds even though they did not.[38]

The basic problem, of course, is that the objective of trying to show what "happened" to a company's profit is a meaningless one. Profits are not a physical "thing" that can be disposed of, retained, or paid out. Profit is the name given to the *change* in a company's net assets that results from selected operating, financing, and investing activities during a period or, as the Accounting Principles Board defined it, "the net increase (net decrease) in owners' equity (assets

---

37. Perry Mason stated that a funds statement "contributes materially to . . . the answers to such questions as. . . . Where did the profits go?" (Mason, "*Cash Flow*" *Analysis*, p. 49). Paton and Paton stated that a funds statement "is designed to . . . indicate what disposition has been made of earnings" (William A. Paton and William A. Paton, Jr., *Corporation Accounts and Statements* (New York: Macmillan, 1955), p. 440). A. B. Carson maintains that "among other things it supplies an answer to the question: 'what happened to the profit?' " (A. B. Carson, "A Source and Application of Funds' Philosophy of Financial Accounting," *Accounting Review*, 24 (April, 1949): 160). Roy A. Foulke argues that it "gives a clear answer to the question of what has become of the net profits" (Roy A. Foulke, *Practical Financial Statement Analysis*, 6th ed. (New York: McGraw-Hill, 1968), p. 474). For other similar examples, see Donald A. Corbin, "Proposals for Improving Funds Statements," p. 398; National Accounting Association Research Report no. 38, *Cash Flow Analysis for Managerial Control* (New York: NAA, 1961), p. 58; David F. Hawkins, *Corporate Financial Reporting*, rev. ed. (Homewood, Ill.: Richard D. Irwin, 1977) and *Intermediate Accounting*, 2d ed. (New York: John Wiley & Sons, 1977), p. 983; and Jay M. Smith, Jr. and K. Fred Skousen, *Intermediate Accounting*, 6th ed. (Englewood Cliffs, N.J.: Prentice-Hall, 1977), p. 682.
38. Moonitz captured the essence of this practice when he described it as "awkward, unnecessary, misleading, and just plain wrong" (Moonitz, "Reporting on the Flow of Funds," p. 381).

minus liabilities) of an enterprise for an accounting period from profit-directed activities."[39]

Profit is measured in money, but it is not an asset. One could, of course, show what "happened" to a company's cash—part of which may have been received as a result of its profit directed activities. A statement of cash receipts and payments would show that. Similarly, since profit directed activities also affect other assets, say quick assets, one could also prepare a statement that shows what "happened" to its quick assets, part of which may have been received as a result of its profit directed activities. But to try to show what "happened" to a company's profits is a meaningless objective; no statement can show that.

Confusion over the relationship between net income and the funds statement also shows up in another way. Many accountants appear to consider the role of the income statement to be that of reporting the effect of operating activities on the financial position of a company, while the role of the funds statement is considered to be that of reporting the results of *other* activities, namely financing and investing activities. The Accounting Principles Board, for example, implied that. In APB Opinion no. 19 it stated "an income statement together with a statement of retained earnings reports results of operations but does not show *other* changes in financial position."[40] A more accurate statement would have been, "an income statement together with a statement of retained earnings reports the results of operating activities and some financing and investing activities on the retained earnings of a company, but it does not show how those activities affect other aspects of financial position, nor does it show how most financing and investing activities affect any of the various aspects of financial position." This distinction is important because designers of financial statements must decide whether the object of attention in a funds statement is a set of activities different from those

---

39. AICPA, APB Statement no. 4, *Basic Concepts and Accounting Principles Underlying Financial Statements of Business Enterprises* (New York: AICPA, 1970), par. 134.
40. AICPA, APB Opinion no. 19, *Reporting Changes in Financial Position* (New York: AICPA, 1971), par. 5 (emphasis added). R. M. Skinner argued that "The income statement combined with the balance sheet summarizes the results of operating transactions that have taken place in a fiscal period. The funds statement accomplishes somewhat the same purpose with respect to financing and investment activities" (Ross M. Skinner, *Accounting Principles: A Canadian Viewpoint* (Toronto: Canadian Institute of Chartered Accountants, 1972), p. 248).

shown on the income statement (for example, those operating, financing, and investing activities that do not affect income), or whether it is to report the effect of all activities (including those reported on the income statement) on a different aspect of financial position (for example, on cash, on working capital, and so forth). One statement cannot do everything.

Evaluation of Current Practice

The Accounting Principles Board did little to clarify the role of the funds statement in the overall financial reporting process in APB Opinion no. 19.

Stated Objectives. The objectives of funds statements stated in APB Opinion no. 19 are (1) to summarize the financing and investing activities of the entity, including the extent to which the enterprise has generated funds from operations during the period, and (2) to complete the disclosure of changes in financial position during the period. Those are specious objectives; superficially they appear to be reasonable, but when analyzed and applied in practice they are unclear, misleading, and unattainable.

The meaning of the first objective is unclear. It begs the question of what effects of financing and investing activities should be summarized. Financing and investing activities, like all business activities, have many different effects. A single transaction may affect cash, working capital, total assets, capital structure, net assets, and so forth. Obviously, not all of those can be portrayed in a single statement, but the opinion is silent about which one or ones should be the object or objects of attention in the statement. It says only that the statement "should be based on a broad concept embracing all changes in financial position" without even saying a broad concept of what! The opinion reflects more than just poor draftsmanship; it reflects the absence of an underlying concept.

The second objective is unattainable. As noted, business activities have many effects. No statement can possibly "complete the disclosure of changes in financial position" or "disclose all important changes in financial position for the period covered." A meaningful statement must focus on a specific aspect or dimension of financial position, such as cash, working capital, net assets, monetary assets, and so forth. As Arthur Stone Dewing pointed out,

No representation of anything in this world can be perfect. It must portray one or more aspects or attributes of the thing represented and neglect or throw into insignificance the other aspects or attributes. This observation is conspicuously true when we are dealing with . . . accounting statements. Such statements must select one or at most a very few aspects of the objects represented and neglect all others—as vital statistics consider only the length of years of a man, neglecting every other aspect of his life or characteristics as a human being.[41]

Even the recommended title of the statement required by APB Opinion no. 19, "a statement of changes in financial position," reflects confusion over the objectives of the statement and its relationship to the income statement. Income statements and funds statements are *both* statements of changes in financial position: They both report the effects of business activities on the financial position of a company. The question that needs to be clarified is what aspects of financial position should be reported on. The title of the statement should reflect that.

Implicit Objectives. Although the stated objectives in APB Opinion no. 19 are specious, a careful reading of the entire opinion suggests that the board was concerned with reporting the effects of *all* business activities (not just financing and investing activities) on at least two and perhaps three different aspects of financial position.

The first was to report changes in some measure of the cash or near-cash resources of a company, that is, changes in some measure of its debt paying ability. A number of specific provisions of the opinion support that view. Paragraph 10 requires that "the Statement should prominently disclose working capital or cash provided from or used by operations for the period." Paragraph 11 states that "the Statement may be in balanced form or in a form expressing the changes in financial position in terms of cash, or cash and temporary investments combined, of all quick assets, or of working capital." Paragraph 14 requires that "outlays for the purchase of long-term assets . . . proceeds from sale (or working capital or cash provided by sale) of long-term assets," and "dividends in cash" all be disclosed.

The second type of change that the board appears to have been concerned with having disclosed was capital structure changes. Capital structure refers to claims on the resources of a business enterprise, including both debt and equity claims. Changes in the size of a

---

41. Arthur Stone Dewing, *The Financial Policy of Corporations*, 5th ed., 2 vols. (New York: Ronald Press, 1953), 1:517.

company's capital structure result from activities such as the borrowing and repayment of debt, sale and repurchase of capital stock, profit directed activities, and cash or property dividends. Changes in the composition of a company's capital structure result from activities such as the conversion of convertible securities into common stock and refinancing operations including the swapping of one type of financial instrument for another in a financial reorganization.

Many changes in the size and composition of a company's capital structure also affect its cash, its working capital, and other measures of debt paying ability, but some of them do not. Evidence that the board was concerned with having changes in the size and composition of a company's capital structure as well as changes in its debt paying ability reported is found in the requirement in paragraph 14 that "the Statement should clearly disclose" activities such as "conversion of long-term debt or preferred stock to common stock," "issuance, redemption, or purchase of capital stock . . . for assets other than cash," and "dividends . . . in kind or other distributions to shareholders." Other evidence of the board's concern with changes in a company's capital structure is found in paragraph 6:

> However, a funds statement based on either the cash or the working capital concept of funds sometimes excludes certain financing and investing activities because they do not directly affect cash or working capital during the period. For example, issuing equity securities to acquire a building is both a financing and investing transaction, but does not affect either cash or working capital. To meet all of its objectives, a funds statement should disclose separately the financing and investing aspects of all significant transactions that affect financial position during a period. These transactions include acquisitions or disposal of property in exchange for debt or equity securities and conversion of long-term debt or preferred stock to common stock.

One of the format provisions of APB Opinion no. 19 is that a funds statement "should begin with income or loss before extraordinary items, if any, and add back (or deduct) items recognized in determining that income or loss which did not use (or provide) working capital or cash during the period." This implies that the board was concerned with having reported the effect of a company's income producing activities on both its capital structure and on some measure of its debt paying ability, because net income is, of course, the effect of profit directed activities on net assets (which is an element of capital structure) and adding back (deducting) items "which did not use (or provide) working capital or cash" produces a figure that shows the effect of those activities on working capital or cash. The board's concern becomes blurred, however, when it states in the same paragraph that the "acceptable alternative procedure" of starting with total revenue that provided working capital or cash and deducting operating costs and expenses that required the outlay of working capital or cash "*gives the same result*" (emphasis added). The alternative procedure gives the same result in the sense that the effect on working capital or cash is the same; it does not give the same result in the sense that the effect of those activities on capital structure is not shown.

The third type of change that the board seems to have been concerned with having reported is changes in a company's long-term assets, such as plant and equipment and long-term investments. Most increases in those assets would, of course, be revealed by a statement that shows only changes in cash or working capital. Some, however, such as those resulting from the issuance of debt or equity securities, would be excluded from that type of statement.

The requirement that the issuance of securities for consideration other than cash or working capital be reported as sources and uses of "funds" appears to have been motivated in part by the desire to disclose changes in long-term assets as well as the desire to disclose changes in a company's capital structure. However, the opinion does not contain similar requirements for transactions that increase long-term assets, but do not either decrease working capital (or other measure of debt paying ability) or increase total capital. Such transactions are unusual, but they do occur. The exchange of a long-term investment in securities for plant and equipment or the exchange of land for securities are examples. The opinion requires that "outlays" for the purchase of long-term assets be disclosed, but whether the term "outlays" embraces or excludes exchanges of that kind is not clear.

In summary, the board may have intended to require the disclosure of all increases in long-term assets, but its intentions are not clear. It certainly gave no indication of any desire to show *decreases* in long-term assets; only the "proceeds from sale (or working capital or cash provided by sale) of long-term assets," not the book value of assets sold, are required to be disclosed.

Conclusions

Changes in all three of the measures of financial position discussed in the last section are clearly of interest to investors, creditors, and other external users of financial statements. Changes in debt paying ability are of such obvious interest to creditors and investors that the matter hardly requires comment; the only issue is which measure of debt paying ability is likely to be most useful. Changes in the size and composition of a company's capital structure are also of interest. One of the most widely used financial ratios in credit analysis is the ratio of debt to equity. That ratio would obviously be affected by changes in the composition of a company's capital structure such as the conversion of debentures into common stock and various kinds of refinancing operations. The nature of those activities and a report of how they affect a company's capital structure would, therefore, also be of interest. Changes in the amount or composition of long-term assets are likely to signal changes in a company's future profits and future cash needs, so that they, too, are likely to be of interest to investors and creditors.

The basic problem with APB Opinion no. 19 is not, therefore, that it requires disclosure of unimportant or irrelevant information, but that it requires too many different types of information to be disclosed on the same statement. The result is a confusing statement. Finney's early objective of providing information useful in evaluating solvency by explaining changes in some measure of a company's debt paying ability has been lost; no longer is it possible to determine why debt paying ability has changed because business activities that affect whatever measure of debt paying ability one chooses, as well as those that do not, are all shown simply as sources and uses of "funds." The more recent (and meritorious) objective of showing changes in a company's capital structure is not accomplished either; activities that affect capital structure as well as those that do not, are all shown simply as sources and uses of "funds." Even changes in plant and equipment are not shown clearly. Increases in plant and equipment can usually be readily determined from the funds statement alone, but the reader interested in an explanation of the *net* change in that account must usually piece together information from a company's beginning and ending balance sheet as well as its funds statement and income statement.

In summary, none of the gaps in financial disclosure that the Accounting Principles Board sought to close in Opinion no. 19 have been closed effectively. In practice, statements of changes in financial position are like the miniature cars one sees packed with people in the circus. Those cars are good for entertainment but they are not a good means of transporting large numbers of people. Similarly, statements of changes in financial position are also packed; they are packed with information but they are not an effective means of communicating that information. To get it all into the "car" the APB has had to redefine "funds" so broadly that it has become a meaningless term, and a funds statement that is based on a meaningless concept of funds and that tries to accomplish too much does not communicate information effectively.

7

Recommended Replacements for the Statement of Changes in Financial Position

Chapter 6 concluded that too many different types of information are included in statements of changes in financial position, or funds statements, with the result that those statements are confusing and do not communicate any information clearly. Since all of the basic types of information that the Accounting Principles Board at least implicitly sought to have disclosed in funds statements are potentially useful if presented clearly, the solution to the problem of the unsatisfactory funds statement is obvious; different statements are needed to report the different types of information now crammed into a single statement. Specifically, three statements are needed: (1) a statement of cash receipts and payments, (2) a statement of financing activities, and (3) a statement of investing activities. Those statements are recommended in this study as replacements for the statement of changes in financial position. They are explained, illustrated, and discussed in this chapter.

Statement of Cash Receipts and Payments

A statement of cash receipts and payments should be presented as one of the statements to replace the statement of changes in financial position.

109

General Rationale. The basic rationale for requiring statements of cash receipts and payments is implicit in much of the discussion in earlier chapters of this study. Funds statements based on changes in a company's working capital were developed during the 1920s when working capital was widely regarded as the principal measure of debt paying ability. Information needs of financial statement users have changed significantly during the last fifty years. Investors and creditors no longer regard working capital as the center of attention in solvency analysis; their principal concern now is the ability of a company to obtain cash in amounts adequate to cover required payments. It follows from this that a statement of past cash receipts and payments would be useful for the same basic reason that historical income statements are useful in predicting the future income of a company; both provide the starting point for predicting future performance.

The need for information about the cash receipts and payments of a company has undoubtedly existed for some time, but two developments in recent years have increased the need for that type of information.

First, increasing complexity of business activity together with refinements in the measurement of income have tended to result in greater disparity between the reported income of companies and the amount of cash provided by their profit directed activities. In a simple enterprise, cash receipts from customers for any given year tend to approximate revenue recognized for that year. Similarly, cash payments to suppliers of goods and services tend to approximate expenses recorded for that period. Net income, therefore, tends to be a good surrogate for cash provided by profit directed activities. However, as credit terms become longer and more complex, as companies substitute more highly specialized and longer lasting plant and equipment for labor, as the planning horizons of companies become longer, and as the recognition of revenue becomes farther removed from the receipt of cash, the leads and lags between revenue and cash receipts and between expenses and cash outlays become longer and more pervasive.[1] As a result, net income may greatly exceed cash provided by profit directed activities in some years, and the reverse may occur in other years. The greater the disparity, the greater is the need to report cash receipts and payments. Although cash provided by profit

---

1. APB Opinion no. 18 requiring use of the equity method of accounting for income from investments in common stock is an excellent example of how far revenue recognition criteria have moved from the old realization test.

directed activities can, of course, be estimated by financial statement users by examining year-to-year changes in a company's balance sheet accounts, that method is not accurate, and it does not highlight the disparity between cash provided by profit directed activities and net income the way reporting cash receipts and payments does. Also, creditors are concerned with the volatility from year to year of the amount of cash provided by profit directed activities; the greater the volatility, the greater a company's need for financial flexibility. If, however, the disparity between a company's reported profit and its cash provided by profit directed activities is substantial and random in nature, investors and creditors are unlikely to be aware of that volatility unless actual cash receipts and payments are reported each year; it cannot be discerned through an examination of the income statement.

Second, the increased rate of inflation in recent years has also increased the need for a statement of cash receipts and payments. During a period of rapid inflation, the amount of cash a company provides by its profit directed activities is usually less than its reported profit, because increased amounts of cash are needed to replace higher priced inventories and because receivables tend to grow as the result of higher selling prices. Under those circumstances, reported income is a poorer indicator of cash provided by profit directed activities, and the need for statements of cash receipts and payments increases.

A statement of changes in financial position tied to working capital changes is an ineffective means of calling attention to the discrepancy between the amount of cash a company provided by its profit directed activities and its reported profit, because cash, receivables, and inventories are lumped together as working capital in that type of statement. The effect on cash is therefore obscured, and it is the effect on cash that gives rise to concern for a company's solvency during a period of rising prices. After noting that Professor Lawson, of the University of Manchester Business School in England, has argued for a "cash flow basis of accounting" on the grounds that, under inflationary conditions, "modern accrual accounting overstates the true income of a corporation," Homer Kripke, a lawyer who writes extensively on accounting issues in leading law journals, commented as follows:

> At first I thought that Lawson's insight probably did not apply in the United States because we have a Statement of Changes in Financial Condition (not used in England) from which anyone can create for himself a cash flow statement. But, in our country, that statement has

gotten away from an emphasis on cash to an emphasis on working capital, and it may be an instrument of deception, accidental or purposive.[2]

The case for requiring statements of cash receipts and payments in place of statements of changes in financial position is further strengthened when the confusion that exists over what statements of changes in financial position really show is considered. Even if statements of changes in financial position simply showed changes in working capital and only changes in working capital, many users would misunderstand them because the term working capital is not well understood and because the purpose of preparing a statement based on working capital is not clear in today's environment. But, when those statements purport to show sources and uses of what one writer referred to as that "question-begging word 'Funds',"[3] it is not surprising to find widespread confusion over what they are meant to show, and it is understandable that the "funds" referred to in those statements are confused with cash or money. The word *funds* is commonly used by accountants and nonaccountants alike as a synonym for cash or money. It is used in funds statement literature to refer to cash, to "all financial resources," as well as to nearly everything in between. The following comment is typical of the way many financial analysts switch back and forth between the terms *funds* and *money* when discussing statements of changes in financial position:

> Investment analysis, which historically has moved from emphasis on the balance sheet to the income statement, now is shifting again to focus on the source and applications of *funds* statement. This little-known and -understood document, published in a company's annual report, provides clues to the most crucial question facing American corporations today. What has been—and might be—the source of *money* to support corporate growth? . . .
>
> Technically, the *funds* statement (often called the statement of changes in financial position) acts as a bridge between the balance sheet and the income statement, measuring how changes in noncurrent assets and liabilities affect working capital; practically, it measures the source of growth *money* and how management has chosen to invest these available *funds*.[4]

---

2. Homer Kripke, "A Search for a Meaningful Securities Disclosure Policy," *Business Lawyer*, 31, no. 1 (November, 1975): 303-304.
3. Harold Rose, "Sources and Uses: A British View," *Journal of Accounting Research*, 12 (Autumn, 1974): 138.
4. Jerrold F. Mulder, "The Funds Statement—More Useful Than the Income Account?" *Investment Strategy*, January, 1975, p. 4 (emphasis added).

Erich A. Helfert is no clearer than the author of the foregoing quote when he describes funds statements in the *Financial Analysts Handbook*:

> The funds flow statement is an expanded analysis of the changes in the balance sheet accounts of a company over time. Not limited to the recognition of revenue, expenses, and costs, the funds flow statement uses the wider concept of funds. Funds are not only the cash results of transactions, but rather the full set of commitments and releases of value caused by management decisions over time. . . .
>
> Wider in scope than the income statement, the funds flow statement is an attempt to visualize management decisions in terms of the impact on the balance sheet and the funds under the control of the enterprise. Answers to such questions as the nature of financing supporting new investment commitments, the relative buildup of working capital versus short term loans, and the coverage of dividends with cash flow become quite visible in this analysis.[5]

Even the editor of the *Journal of Accountancy* appears to have been confused over what funds statements are supposed to show. At the time APB Opinion no. 3 recommended presentation of a funds statement based on the "all financial resources" concept of funds,[6] an editorial in the *Journal of Accountancy* suggested that "the best way to make [cash flow] understandable, surely, is by furnishing the source and application of funds statement recommended by the APB."[7]

Marshall S. Armstrong, past chairman of the Financial Accounting Standards Board, commented recently as follows:

> While I attribute the current surge of activity in the accounting arena to the loss of confidence in business, I must say, that in part I feel that traditional accounting has failed to communicate. It has failed because of arcane language, and abstract and elusive concepts.[8]

Surely one of the most abstract and elusive concepts used in accounting today is that of "funds." Over ten years ago, Robert T. Sprouse,

---

5. Erich A. Helfert, *Financial Analysts Handbook I*, ed. Sumner N. Levine (Homewood, Ill.: Dow Jones-Irwin, 1975), pp. 593-594.
6. AICPA, APB Opinion no. 3, *Statement of Source and Application of Funds* (New York: AICPA, 1963), par. 9.
7. "Not to Mislead the Public," *Journal of Accountancy*, 118 (July, 1964): 24.
8. Quoted in Financial Accounting Standards Board, *Status Report*, no. 41, October 12, 1976, p. 2.

now vice chairman of the Financial Accounting Standards Board, criticized the term *funds* and observed, "Since funds seem to mean all things to all people, it is probably time to put that term on the scrap heap along with 'surplus' and 'reserve'."[9] The meaning of the term *funds* has undoubtedly become even more confused than when Sprouse made that comment. One of the principal advantages of a statement of cash receipts and payments is that it would be readily understood by both its preparers and its users. Furthermore, calling it a statement of cash receipts and payments, not a funds flow statement or statement of changes in financial position, and labelling the totals on it cash receipts and cash payments rather than sources and uses of funds, would go a long way towards relegating the word *funds* to the scrap heap where it belongs. That, in itself, would improve communication and dispel much of the confusion over the relationships between business activities, profits, and changes in financial position discussed in chapter 6.

Users' Views. During the 1950s and 1960s, when funds statements started to come into widespread use in published annual reports, they were enthusiastically received by many financial statement users.[10] The financial press published many comments by financial analysts praising the usefulness of the new "third" financial statement and encouraging companies to "get in line" by including funds statements in their annual reports. In fact, when APB Opinion no. 3 was issued in 1962, the Financial Analysts Federation adopted a policy paper putting that organization on record as favoring the inclusion of funds statements in reports to shareholders, and the president of the New York Stock Exchange, in a much publicized move, strongly

---

9. Robert T. Sprouse, "The Measurement of Financial Position and Income: Purpose and Procedure," Paper no. 7, *Research in Accounting Management*, ed. Robert K. Jaedicke, Yuji Ijiri, and Oswald Nielsen (New York: American Accounting Association, 1966), p. 104.
10. See, for example, the comments of several financial analysts quoted in Charles T. Horngren, "Increasing the Utility of Financial Statements," *Journal of Accountancy*, 108 (July, 1959): 40. Based on his survey of financial analysts, Horngren concluded, that "the results of the questionnaire certainly indicate that a funds statement, which now appears in a few annual reports, should be universally adopted as a required financial report," p. 41. See also "Comments on 'Cash Flow' Analysis and the Funds Statement," *Journal of Accountancy*, 114 (September, 1962): 63-64.

urged all listed companies to include funds statements in their annual reports.[11]

It is important that that enthusiastic praise for funds statements be viewed in its proper context and that it not be interpreted as support for funds statements based on working capital as opposed to statements of cash receipts and payments. Before the widespread adoption in practice of funds statements in the 1950s and 1960s, no statement that even attempted to portray changes in any measure of a company's debt paying ability was generally available to financial statement users. Consequently, it is not surprising that, at least initially, many analysts were not very critical of the exact form of the newly available funds statement. The important point to them was that accountants had finally recognized that *some* statement was needed to report information not found in balance sheets and income statements and they probably would have supported almost any form of funds statement. Furthermore, as noted above, there was, and still is, widespread confusion over what is meant by the term *funds*, and many analysts apparently believe that funds statements of the type typically found in practice today do show a company's "cash flows."[12]

When the distinction between funds statements based on changes in working capital or other broad concepts of funds on the one hand and cash flow statements or statements of cash receipts and payments on the other has been explicitly recognized, users have almost uniformly expressed a preference for statements based on cash rather than working capital flows. For example, Frank J. Hoenemeyer, an insurance executive, stated:

> From our standpoint [the] importance and usefulness [of funds statements based on working capital] have been somewhat overemphasized. To a large extent, we feel we can get the information we want without

---

11. In 1962, shortly after the AICPA published Perry Mason's study of funds statements (Accounting Research Study no. 2), Philip L. West, vice president of the New York Stock Exchange, stated in a letter to the AICPA Accounting Principles Board, "I . . . hope that the recommendation that the funds statement be treated as a major financial statement will be adopted by the Institute. If this is done, we will urge listed companies to include such statements in their reports to stockholders, as we believe this will be a big step forward in financial reporting" ("Comments on 'Cash Flow' Analysis and the Funds Statement," *Journal of Accountancy*, 114 (September, 1962): 64). See also, "Not to Mislead the Public," *Journal of Accountancy*, 118 (July, 1964): 23-24.
12. See, for example, the comments of Mulder, "The Funds Statement," and Helfert, *Financial Analysts Handbook*.

the use of the funds statement. We are interested in seeing what has brought about . . . changes in cash, though. This is of more interest to us than changes in working capital.[13]

A report by the National Association of Accountants of a field study of the attitudes about cash flow information of financial managers stated:

> In contrast with cash flow statements, company representatives interviewed generally expressed the opinion that statements of sources and applications of working capital have comparatively little usefulness to management.
>
> The field study shows that top management is strongly interested in the amount of cash generated by operations and the underlying information showing sources and application of the cash flow.
>
> In addition, company representatives interviewed commented that investment analysts and sophisticated investors are usually interested in cash flow data.[14]

---

13. Frank J. Hoenemeyer, executive vice president, the Prudential Insurance Company of America, quoted in Thomas J. Burns, ed., *The Use of Accounting Data in Decision Making*, College of Commerce and Administration Monograph no. AA1 (Columbus: Ohio State University, 1966), pp. 57-58. See also a similar comment by Hoenemeyer on p. 90 where he notes that a "statement of change in cash position . . . permits a better analysis of receivable and inventory requirements [than a funds statement] and focuses on the determination of the minimum cash balance needed to run the business."

14. National Association of Accountants, *Cash Flow Analysis for Managerial Control*, NAA Research Report 38 (New York: National Association of Accountants, 1961), pp. 58-60. This study also contains some interesting observations about funds statements based on working capital. The following comment is described as typical of those made by those financial managers interviewed: "A statement of source and application of funds in working capital form has been included among financial statements received by top executives for at least twenty-five years. Those who receive it understand it very well, but the use they make of it is questionable. They probably use it very little" (p. 58).

The author of the study, apparently bothered by the contradiction of the widespread publication of funds statements based on working capital in external reporting, and the nearly unanimous rejection of that form of statement by those he interviewed (financial managers), found it necessary to use the old rationale that current assets are a measure of the cash that will be available to pay current liabilities (see discussion in chapter 2 of this study) to explain this dilemma. He observed, "On the other hand, the creditor (especially the short term creditor) is understandably interested in measures of security. The amount of assets which, in the course of operations, will be converted into cash in a

Richard D. Bradish found a similar interest among financial analysts interviewed by him in a 1965 study:

> While fund-flow analysis reflects most of the changes in noncurrent items of a balance sheet over time, cash-flow analysis also includes changes in current assets and current liabilities. Because the latter is believed to provide more useful information, financial analysts have come to place increasing stress on the importance of cash flows in their analysis . . . Most analysts interviewed would like to see the cash flow statement used by every company publishing financial data.[15]

Bradish's findings were confirmed recently by the Advisory Committee on Corporate Disclosure to the SEC. It reported as follows:

> The Committee has been impressed with the importance attributed by financial statement users to understanding the history of a firm's cash flow in order to predict the amounts, timing, and uncertainties of future cash flows. . . .
> Both equity and bond analysts interviewed by the staff indicated their interest in the following questions:
> 1. How much cash was earned from operations . . . ?*
> 2. To what extent was the enterprise able to finance debt principal and interest payments, dividends on common and preferred stock, and capital expenditures from internally generated cash flow?

*Some security analysts would recommend changing the Statement of Changes in Financial Position to reconcile to cash instead of to working capital.[16]

One of the members of the Advisory Committee on Corporate Disclosure to the SEC, Roger F. Murray, professor of finance, noted several years earlier that one of the lessons to be learned from the Penn Central collapse is that

> Conventional measures of capacity to pay debt may be seriously deficient. . . . New analytical techniques need to be developed from

comparatively short time is a measure of the amount of cash which will be available to pay debts, and the excess of such current assets over current liabilities is an important index of the creditor's margin of safety" (p. 5).
15. Richard D. Bradish, "Corporate Reporting and the Financial Analyst," *Accounting Review*, 40 (October, 1965): 761, 762.
16. Report of the Advisory Committee on Corporate Disclosure to the Securities and Exchange Commission, printed for the use of the House Committee on Interstate and Foreign Commerce, 95th Cong., 1st Sess., Committee Print 95-29, November 3, 1977, pp. 503-504.

the skeleton form of the source and application of funds statement. What may be required for analytical purposes is a conversion of statements prepared on the accrual basis into statements prepared on the cash basis for complicated structures like the Penn Central.[17]

Bankers, too, would like to know the cash flow of loan applicants. Walter B. Wriston, chairman of the board of Citibank, N.A., stated in a speech before Peat, Marwick, Mitchell & Co. personnel—

> When I came into the banking business, we were asset conscious and we loaned money on that basis. Well, assets give you a warm feeling, but they don't generate cash. The first question I would ask any borrower these days is, "What is your breakeven cash flow?" That's the one thing we can't find out from your audit reports and it's the single most important question we ask. It's important that you figure out a way to present the difference between real cash flow and accrual cash flow.[18]

Still further evidence of interest in a company's cash flows is found in the many references to "cash flow" or "cash flow per share" in investment literature and in the "cash flow" data often included in corporate annual reports. Much of that data is misleading; much of it is calculated incorrectly so that it is not really a measure of cash provided by profit directed activities (or any other definable set of activities for that matter); and, even if it were correctly calculated, it is often used to support unwarranted inferences concerning the performance of management and the value of a company's stock.[19]

---

17. Roger F. Murray, "The Penn Central Debacle: Lessons for Financial Analysis," *Journal of Finance*, 26, no. 2 (May, 1971): 332.
18. *World* (Peat, Marwick, Mitchell & Co.), Spring, 1974, p. 49. Wriston's views were echoed recently by John Ingraham, vice president of Citibank (New York), in an interview with *Forbes Magazine* (July 1, 1975, p. 71):

    "When a company gets in this condition [in financial trouble], out the window go all the fancy bookkeeping concepts: It's just a basic 'How much cash is coming in versus how much cash is going out.'"

    For further discussion of bankers' interests in cash flow data, see Morton Backer, *Financial Reporting for Security Investment and Credit Decisions* (New York: National Association of Accountants, 1970), pp. 51-52.
19. For further discussion of some of the ways this information is used see, for example, William A. Paton, "The 'Cash Flow' Illusion," *Accounting Review*, 38 (April, 1963): 243-251; Loyd C. Heath, "Calculation and Meaning of Cash Flow in Security Analysis," *Financial Analysts Journal*, 18, no. 5 (September-October, 1962): 65-67; and Robert K. Jaedicke and Robert T. Sprouse, *Accounting Flows: Income, Funds and Cash* (Englewood Cliffs, N.J.: Prentice-Hall, 1965), pp. 115-126. See also SEC Accounting Series Release no. 142, *Reporting Cash Flow and Other Related Data*, March 15, 1973.

A conclusion that all such information is provided with the intent to deceive, however, would be unwarranted. At least some of it undoubtedly reflects a genuine concern to provide useful information about the cash flows of a company, but because of the widespread confusion about the relationship between business activities, profits, and cash flows discussed in chapter 6, the message does not always come through clearly. While some of the blame for this can no doubt be laid at the feet of those who supply cash flow information (some suppliers *do* intend to deceive), some of the blame can also be laid at the feet of accountants.

Accountants' Views. The accounting profession has not tried to counter the misunderstanding and confusion surrounding a company's cash flows by requiring a readily understood statement that shows clearly where a company's cash comes from, and the purposes for which it is paid out. As noted in chapter 1, interest in cash flow information has often been interpreted as a challenge to the supremacy of the income statement and contemptuously dismissed. To make matters worse, the profession has continued to require funds statements that have reinforced many of the misconceptions that gave rise to the misleading data it condemned. For example, the practice of adding depreciation to net income and labelling the total "funds provided by operations" has done little to counter the common misconception that depreciation is a source of cash.

Not all accountants, however, believe that cash flow information is misleading. Arthur L. Thomas believes that

> One's reaction to cash flow accounting *should* be similar to one's reaction to "bootleg" bookkeeping (which it resembles): as a symptom of possible inadequacies in the "official" system, not as something reprehensible.[20]

Many accountants agree with Thomas' position and argue that some type of statement that discloses the amounts and timing of a company's past cash flows should be presented on the grounds that past cash flows are useful in predicting future cash flows. The AICPA Study Group on the Objectives of Financial Statements, for example,

---

20. Arthur L. Thomas, *The Allocation Problem in Financial Accounting Theory* (Evanston, Ill.: American Accounting Association, 1969), p. 101 (emphasis original). Allan R. Drebin views "cash flowitis" as a symptom or "syndrome" of a more serious malady, "information anemia" (Allan R. Drebin, "'Cash Flowitis': Malady or Syndrome?" *Journal of Accounting Research*, 2 (Spring, 1964): 25-34).

noted that one of the objectives of financial statements is "to provide information useful to investors and creditors for predicting, comparing, and evaluating potential cash flows to them in terms of amount, timing, and related uncertainty."[21] It then went on to explain that

> The measurements made by accounting should relate to the enterprise's goal of producing the most cash for its owners. These measurements, therefore, should emphasize the *actual* or prospective disbursement or receipt of cash. Users need to know about probable cash movements of an enterprise to estimate cash flows to them.[22]

Several years earlier, George J. Staubus used a similar line of reasoning to explain the rationale of providing investors with cash flow data:

> If the investor expects cash transfer from the firm, he must predict the firm's cash balance (a useful measure of capacity to pay) at the future date or dates in which he is interested. Since a future cash balance at any particular date is determined by the present cash balance and cash receipts and disbursements between now and the future date, investors are interested in predicting the firm's future cash flows. Past recurring cash flows provide a starting point for predicting future recurring cash flows.[23]

The views expressed by J. W. Giese and T. P. Klammer in a 1974 article reflect the views of many accountants:

> Besides mixing financing and investing activities with operational flows, the working capital concept implies that working capital is a liquid resource. In a going concern, accounts receivable and inventory are as necessary as plant and equipment. Granted there is a minimum requirement for cash as well, but cash represents the only discretionary resource available to management. Besides, nearly everyone understands cash! Confusion continues to exist over the use of the term "working capital" among trained financial analysts and accountants.

---

21. AICPA, *Objectives of Financial Statements*, Report of the Study Group on the Objectives of Financial Statements (New York: AICPA, 1973), p. 20.
22. AICPA, *Objectives of Financial Statements*, p. 22 (emphasis added).
23. George J. Staubus, "Alternative Asset Flow Concepts," *Accounting Review*, 41 (July, 1966): 407.

Thus, the cash approach permits a more informative disclosure of the effects of operations and the investing and financing activities.[24]

Measuring the income of a complex business enterprise involves a multitude of necessarily arbitrary and subjective allocations. Statements of cash receipts and payments, on the other hand, do not require the use of arbitrary allocations. As many accountants have recognized, cash flows can be measured objectively. David Solomons, for example, argued that

> Though no accounting statement is immune to criticism, the statement of sources and uses of funds represents a happier union of objectivity and relevance than any of the others. This is not to say that it is free from distortion. For example, in a statement drawn up to show movements of net working capital, the use of LIFO as the basis of inventory valuation will, if the level of inventory is not stable, introduce the same distortion into the funds statement as it does into the other accounting statements. The same is true of any other procedure which depends on the valuation of current assets. A statement of *cash* flows is free from these disturbing influences or, if they are present, they are openly present. For this reason, it seems to me, anyone using accounting data is likely to find a statement of cash flows one of the most useful of accounting statements, and more useful than any other variant of the funds statement.[25]

Staubus argued similarly

> The cash flow concept requires use of only the most impeccable of measurement methods—counting the face value of money. This method

---

24. J. W. Giese and T. P. Klammer, "Achieving the Objectives of APB Opinion no. 19," *Journal of Accountancy*, 137 (March, 1974): 57. John W. Coughlan, one of the most outspoken critics of working capital, expressed similar views ten years earlier. After observing that funds statements based on working capital changes have "baffled a generation of accounting students" and that "it is therefore hardly conceivable that [they have] enlightened stockholders and other lay readers," he argued, "Working capital has been thought of as a "pool" of resources available to satisfy the claims of short term creditors. But it is unlikely that any banker or creditor will slake his thirst from any part of the pool other than the cash portion. Many a firm has been known to pay its debts with cash, but not one has drawn a check on working capital. Working capital, *per se*, has no bearing on short term credit standing, and it is only useful for whatever implication it may have for cash and cash flow" (John W. Coughlan, "Funds and Income," *NAA Bulletin*, September, 1964, pp. 24-25).
25. David Solomons, quoted in Burns, ed., *Use of Accounting Data in Decision Making*, p. 23 (emphasis original).

can be applied with great accuracy, and it measures a quality—present purchasing power—that is highly relevant to the managers and investors who may be using the data to make a decision.[26]

Eldon S. Hendriksen carried this argument even further. After explaining that cash flows are the raw data on which nearly all accounting measurements are based, he argued that

> Because of the deliberate and inherent biases created by the use of allocation procedures and historical transaction prices, there is some doubt that traditional accounting methods are adequate to report the complex economic activities of today. One way of avoiding some of these biases is to emphasize the reporting of cash flows, supplemented by other information and appropriate classifications, to permit the users of financial statements to make their own predictions regarding the future.[27]

Accounting textbooks are usually limited to discussions of the state of the art in accounting. They usually are not, and they are not expected to be, on the leading edge of new accounting thought. They seldom criticize or even seriously question the accepted rationale for current practice. The authors of one leading intermediate accounting text, however, apparently found it so difficult to explain the rationale underlying statements of changes in financial position based on a working capital concept of "funds" that they recently argued that cash flow statements should replace statements of changes in financial position:

> Although a statement of changes in financial position prepared on a "working capital" basis as discussed in the first part of this chapter serves useful purposes, similar statements prepared on a "cash flow" basis generally are considerably more relevant both for internal management and the investor. Clearly, cash, as opposed to the concept of working capital, is more commonly understood by management and the investor alike. Also, all working capital problems "come to rest" in the cash position. A statement of changes in financial position prepared on the cash basis would preclude the need for a similar statement on the working capital basis although the opposite is not the case. . . . . In Opinion 19 the APB was very careful to specify that the state of changes in financial position could be presented either on a working capital or cash basis. Unfortunately, the board did not specifically recognize the obviously greater relevance of the cash flow approach.[28]

---

26. Staubus, "Asset Flow Concepts," p. 411.
27. Eldon S. Hendriksen, *Accounting Theory*, 3d ed. (Homewood, Ill.: Richard D. Irwin, 1977), p. 242.
28. Glenn A. Welsch, Charles T. Zlatkovich, and John Arch White, *Intermediate Accounting*, 3d ed. (Homewood, Ill.: Richard D. Irwin, 1972), p. 1016.

Perhaps the principal concern of accountants over the presentation of cash flow statements is that cash flow is subject to manipulation by management. Davidson, Schindler, and Weil, for example, argued that cash flow statements are "unsatisfactory" for external reporting because "If, for whatever reason, a firm wanted to show an increase in funds for the end of a period . . . it need only borrow cash for one or two days."[29]

The fallacy in that argument is that it is based on an implicit assumption that financial statement users consider only the total or gross cash receipts without regard to where that cash came from. The significance of any financial data will undoubtedly be misunderstood by some users, but the potential danger that a statement of cash receipts and payments will confuse them is miniscule compared to the confusion and misunderstanding that has been fostered by the broad concepts of funds advocated by Davidson, Schindler, and Weil and others as a way of avoiding management manipulation. A measure of debt paying ability that is relevant to the information needs of users of financial statements that is easily understood, that can be objectively measured, and yet cannot be manipulated by management to deceive persons unfamiliar with business practices is an unattainable goal.

In summary, a strong case can be made for requiring a statement of cash receipts and payments for external financial reporting. Analysis of financial statement users' needs leads to that conclusion, and it is supported by the arguments of both financial statement users themselves as well as by those of many accountants who have written on the subject recently.

Illustration of Recommended Statement of Cash Receipts and Payments. The form of the statement of cash receipts and payments recommended in this study is illustrated and explained in this section. This illustration gives an overall view of the nature of the information that should be included in such a statement, but it is not exhaustive. Experimentation and further study will undoubtedly be needed before resolving all of the issues raised by this new form of statement.

An income statement (exhibit 7-1), a statement of retained earnings (exhibit 7-2), a statement of cash receipts and payments (exhibit 7-3), and a supporting schedule (exhibit 7-4) illustrating calculation of

---

29. Sidney Davidson, James S. Schindler, and Roman L. Weil, *Fundamentals of Accounting*, 5th ed. (Hinsdale, Ill.: Dryden Press, 1975), pp. 574-575.

cash provided by operations are presented for Example, Inc. The related balance sheets of Example, Inc., for December 31, 1977, and December 31, 1976, are presented in chapter 5 (exhibit 5-1). The income statement and the statement of retained earnings are presented only to show the relationship of the statement of cash receipts and payments to those statements.

Cash receipts and payments only. Only business activities that affected cash are shown on the statement of cash receipts and payments. If financing and investing activities that did not affect cash are shown on the statement as if they did, users will become confused about what the statement shows. Financing transactions that did not affect cash should be shown on a statement of financing activities; investing transactions that did not affect cash should be shown on a statement of investing activities.

Separate schedule of operations. For the purpose of clarity of presentation, details of cash provided by profit-directed activities or what are called operations (to simplify terminology on the statement) are shown on a separate schedule rather than on the face of the statement of cash. Both the absolute magnitude of many of the cash receipts and payments from operations, such as the amount of cash collected from customers and the amount paid for merchandise, as well as the many types of cash payments, tend to overshadow some of the other figures on the statement of cash receipts and payments, such as cash borrowed and fixed assets purchased, which may be of greater significance to the financial statement user in estimating future cash receipts and payments.

Cash provided by operations. The schedule of cash provided by operations illustrates the direct (as opposed to the indirect) method of calculating that amount. By using the direct method, the schedule shows the actual sources and uses of cash. If the indirect method were used, the schedule would start with net income and adjust that figure for all revenues and expenses that did not affect cash. Those are the two alternative methods of presenting funds provided by operations in statements of changes in financial position that the Accounting Principles Board described as acceptable in APB Opinion no. 19.

Exhibit 7-1

Example, Inc.
INCOME STATEMENT
FOR YEAR ENDING
DECEMBER 31, 1977

Revenues		
Sales		$791,293
Other income		2,605
		793,898
Costs and expenses		
Cost of sales		436,644
Administrative and selling expenses (including depreciation of $30,580)	$297,679	
Interest expense	6,941	
Other expenses	18,901	760,165
Income before taxes on income		33,733
Income tax expense		
Current	14,133	
Deferred	2,059	16,192
Net income		$ 17,541

Exhibit 7-2

Example, Inc.
STATEMENT OF RETAINED EARNINGS
FOR YEAR ENDING DECEMBER 31, 1977

Retained earnings 12/31/76			$32,609
Net income for 1977		$17,541	
Less: Dividends on preferred	$ 3,000		
Dividends on common	10,558	13,558	3,983
Retained earnings 12/31/77			$36,592

Exhibit 7-3

Example, Inc.
**STATEMENT OF CASH RECEIPTS AND PAYMENTS
FOR YEAR ENDING DECEMBER 31, 1977**

Cash balance 12/31/76		$15,666
Sources of cash:		
Cash provided by operations (Schedule 1)	$27,537	
Sale of marketable securities	3,062	
Sale of land, buildings, and equipment	12,793	
Net amount borrowed	31,092	
Received from issuance of common stock	7,495	81,979
Cash available		97,645
Uses of cash:		
Purchase of land, buildings, and equipment	62,119	
Payment of dividends	13,558	75,677
Cash balance 12/31/77		$21,968

Exhibit 7-4

Schedule 1
Cash Provided by Operations

Cash collected from customers		$783,545
Interest and dividends received		1,417
Total cash receipts from operations		784,962
Cash disbursements:		
For merchandise inventories	$457,681	
For administrative and selling expenses	264,577	
For interest	6,941	
For other expenses	14,953	
For taxes	13,273	757,425
Cash provided by operations		$ 27,537

The indirect method is basically a set of work sheet adjustments rather than an explanation of how operating activities affected cash. It is analogous to calculating income by subtracting stockholders' equity at the beginning of the year from stockholders' equity at the end of the year, then adjusting the difference from nonincome items, such as dividends and purchases and sales of capital stock. That method will, of course, work if the proper adjustments are made, but if accountants were to prepare income statements in that way, it seems likely that many financial statement users would be confused. They would begin to describe dividends, for example, as a "source" of profits the same way they now describe depreciation as a "source" of funds because they are both "add-backs" when the indirect method of calculation is used. The indirect method of calculating cash provided by operations is pernicious because it is almost certain to continue to confuse financial statement users by reinforcing the incredible notion that profits and depreciation are sources of cash. The direct method, on the other hand, is likely to be useful in dispelling some of the confusion that now exists over the relationship between business activities and cash receipts and payments, because it shows clearly that profits are neither cash nor a source of cash, that cash comes from customers, that it is paid for merchandise, administrative and selling expenses, taxes, and so forth, and that depreciation is neither a source nor a use of cash.[30]

Financial statement users are interested in past cash receipts and payments primarily because past receipts and payments are likely to be useful in estimating future receipts and payments. Users, therefore, would like to know whether cash receipts and payments from operations reported on the statement of cash receipts and payments provides a reliable basis for estimating what is likely to occur in the future.

A company's cash receipts and payments from operations can, of course, be manipulated by management. A statement of cash receipts and payments cannot, therefore, be used blindly. It is a useful statement in the hands of sophisticated users, but it does not provide simple answers to complex questions. The failure to replace inventory, delaying payment of operating liabilities, accelerating collection

---

30. In commenting on Perry Mason's study of funds statements in 1962, Andrew Barr, former chief accountant of the Securities and Exchange Commission, argued in favor of the indirect method because he felt that use of the direct method would give "an appearance of constructing an income statement on two bases" and that the indirect method "is more likely to discourage the notion that [depreciation] may be ignored in the determination of income" ("Comments on 'Cash Flow' Analysis and the Funds Statement," *Journal of Accountancy*, 114 (September, 1962): 66). These are not strong arguments. Presentation of a schedule of cash provided by operations would lead to increased understanding of net income measured by the accrual method rather than confusion of the two measures. The point that depreciation is an expense that must be deducted from revenue to determine net income is a well-settled issue in accounting today which would not be disturbed by presentation of a statement of cash receipts and payments.

of accounts receivable, and so forth, all tend to increase cash provided by operations. Consequently, actual cash provided from operations for any given year may be a poor measure of normal or recurring receipts and payments. Although income may be less susceptible to manipulation, there are many opportunities for accelerating or retarding reported income, and the same basic criticism is, therefore, applicable to both income and cash provided by operations. Analysts know that when estimating a company's future earning power they must examine its reported income for several past years rather than just a single year and they must analyze each year's income in an effort to determine whether it is the result of nonrecurring or unusual events, regardless of whether any elements of income fit the criteria for extraordinary items set forth in APB Opinion no. 30. Similarly, analysts should know that a company's cash provided by operations for any one year can be manipulated, and they will, therefore, need to examine changes in inventories, receivables, operating liabilities, and so forth, to determine their impact on this year's cash provided by operations before assuming it will be repeated next year.

Since a company's cash provided by operations must be evaluated in the light of changes in its inventory, receivables, operating liabilities, and so forth, the argument might be made that a statement showing the indirect method of calculating cash provided by operations would be more useful than a statement showing the direct method because changes in those assets and liabilities that affect a company's cash provided by operations would appear on the indirect type statement. This argument has some validity, but the arguments in favor of the direct method outweigh it. The confusion surrounding the relationships between business activities, profits, and cash receipts and payments are deep-seated, serious, and pervasive.[31] An easily understood statement that helps clarify these relationships is badly needed and, as noted above, a statement based on the indirect method will only further confuse. Sophisticated users know that information concerning changes in inventories, receivables, and so forth,

---

31. Spiller and Virgil reported that "almost 45 percent of the sample firms conveyed the impression that they had acquired capital assets with depreciation money, financed growth through depreciation, or engaged in similar forms of black magic" (Earl A. Spiller and Robert L. Virgil, "Effectiveness of APB Opinion 19 in Improving Funds Reporting," *Journal of Accounting Research*, 12 (Spring, 1974): 131). For further discussion of some of the ways this confusion is manifest in corporate reports, see William J. Vatter, "Operating Confusion in Accounting—Two Reports or One?" *Journal of Business*, 36, no. 3 (July, 1963): 190-298.

is available to them in the beginning and ending balance sheet accounts; they need only subtract the ending balance of an account from the beginning of that account to determine the net change for the year. Unsophisticated users are unlikely to understand the indirect type statement; it will only reinforce their mistaken beliefs about where cash comes from.

A third possibility, of course, would be to present two schedules, one based on the direct and the other on the indirect method of calculation, but that, too, has great potential for further confusing users and, therefore, should not be adopted.

Operating vs. nonoperating activities. Distinguishing between operating and nonoperating activities on a statement of cash receipts and payments is, in some ways, similar to the problem of distinguishing between ordinary and extraordinary items on an income statement. Both distinctions are useful, but there are no readily identifiable operational criteria that can be used for making either of them. They are both problems of drawing lines on a continuum, and opinions of reasonable persons will always differ on where such lines should be drawn. If statements of cash receipts and payments are required, refinement of the distinction between operating and nonoperating activities will probably be one of the major implementation problems.

Two types of items have, in effect, been "pulled out" of the cash provided by operations on the financial statements of Example, Inc., and have been treated separately as nonoperating activities on the statement of cash receipts and payments rather than including them in the cash provided by operations. These are the sale of marketable securities and the purchase and sale of land, buildings, and equipment. The cash effects of the purchase and sale of inventories, on the other hand, are included in cash provided by operations.

The purchase and sale of all three types of assets could be reported in the same way on the statement of cash receipts and payments. The purchase and sale of inventories is the same type of activity as the purchase and sale of marketable securities and fixed assets in the sense that they are all usually considered part of the normal part of the normal operating activities of a business enterprise, and current generally accepted accounting principles require that the income effects of all of them be reported as ordinary as opposed to extraordinary income.

The case for treating the purchase and sale of marketable securities and fixed assets differently from the purchase and sale of inventories must, therefore, be made on the grounds that they are of different significance to those interested in the cash receipts and payments of a business enterprise. The purchase and sale of fixed assets are of special significance because they are of relatively infrequent occurrence, because they are often relatively large in amount, and because management is likely to have more control over the timing of them than it does over the purchase and sale of merchandise inventory. The purchase and sale of marketable securities are also of special significance because these transactions probably indicate a surplus or shortage of cash on hand at the time they were entered into, and because they, too, are likely to occur infrequently and be significant in amount.

Nonetheless, distinguishing between the items that should be included in the cash flow from operations and the items that should be reported separately on the face of the statement of cash receipts and payments is likely to be troublesome. The criteria used for classifying the income effects of business activities as ordinary or extraordinary are not likely to be useful in deciding whether the cash effects of those activities should be included in or excluded from a company's cash provided by operations because the problems are different. The fact that income measurement and reporting issues have dominated accounting thinking for so long should not be allowed to obscure the fundamental nature of the cash flow problem.

Statement of Financing Activities

A statement of financing activities should be presented as the second statement to replace the statement of changes in financial position.

General Rationale. A statement of cash receipts and payments alone would not accomplish all of the objectives of APB Opinion no. 19. The board was concerned with the effect of business activities on the size and composition of a company's capital structure and on its long-term assets as well as how those activities affected its debt paying ability. The second statement recommended in this study, the statement of financing activities, is designed to achieve the second of those objectives, disclosure of the effects of business activities on the capital structure of a company.

The statement of financing activities would be similar in format to the recommended statement of cash receipts and payments. It would explain changes in a company's capital structure in much the same way that a cash flow statement explains changes in its cash position. It would, however, include changes within a company's capital structure (for example, conversion of securities into common stock) as well as changes in the total amount of its capital structure. The term capital structure is used here to refer to a company's financing liabilities and its stockholders' equity. Profits and dividends as well as financing activities more narrowly defined, such as borrowing and repayment of debt and purchase and sale of capital stock, all affect capital structure and would, therefore, be shown on the statement of financing activities.

Many business activities that affect a company's capital structure, such as borrowing money, repayment of debt, issuance of capital stock, and payment of dividends also affect its cash position and would, therefore, appear on its statement of cash receipts and payments as well as on its statement of financing activities. While this might at first appear to be duplicate reporting of those activities, it is not. Different effects of them would be reported on each of the two statements. The statement of cash receipts and payments would report their effects on cash, whereas the statement of financing activities would report their effects on capital structure. This is necessary to keep both statements clear, simple, and understandable. The alternative, of course, is to design a statement that reports both effects on a single statement. That is what the Accounting Principles Board tried to do in APB Opinions nos. 3 and 19. It cannot be done in a way that both the objectives of the statement as well as the information reported on it are clear and understandable to financial statement users.

Illustration of Statement of Financing Activities. A statement of financing activities for Example, Inc., is presented in exhibit 7-5. It articulates with the other financial statements of Example, Inc., presented in this chapter and in chapter 5.

The focus of attention in the statement of financing activities is on all major financing activities—that is, all activities that affect its capital structure, regardless of whether those activities involve the exchange of securities or other financing instruments (for example, notes, leases, and stock options) for cash, for services, for noncash assets, or simply the exchange of one type of financing instrument for another. Some activities that have a financing dimension will not be reported on this statement. The purchase of merchandise on credit, for example, has a financing dimension, but it does not affect a company's capital structure. Financing activities were defined as changes in capital structure to focus attention on those activities entered into for the primary purpose of providing financing as opposed to those that arise out of or are incidental to a company's operating activities. That distinction is useful even though drawing such a line must be somewhat arbitrary.

Two types of financing. The statement of financing activities distinguishes between debt financing and equity financing. The debt financing section reconciles with the financing liabilities section of the balance sheet shown in chapter 5 (exhibit 5-1). The equity financing section reconciles with the stockholders' equity section of that balance sheet and separately shows changes in convertible preferred, common stock, and capital in excess of par value and retained earnings.

Construction of the statement. Since the net increase in debt financing ties in with the change in financing liabilities, everything that affects the total amount of financing liabilities must be included on the statement of financial activities. Some changes, such as amortization of premiums or discount on bonds payable, may, of course, be immaterial in amount. To avoid cluttering up the statement, they should be lumped together under "other changes" or a similar description.

The statement should show both increases and decreases in each type of debt instrument during the year such as is shown for notes payable to banks in the Example, Inc., statement. For example, the fact that a company engaged in extensive short-term financing during the year may be regarded as significant by some financial statement users even though there was little or no net change in that liability. It indicates a dependence on obtaining credit that, if jeopardized, could have serious implications. Although not shown on the statement illustrated, it might be useful to describe briefly the rate of interest and other significant terms of any new financing either on the face of the statement or in notes. These and other details of presentation need to be considered carefully before requiring the presentation of this type of statement.

The equity financing section of the statement of financing activities is similar in many respects to the debt financing section and similar procedures should apply. Not only does the net increase in equity financing tie in with the stockholders' equity section of the balance sheet, but also the change in each of its major components—convertible preferred, common stock, capital in excess of par value, and retained earnings ties in with the corresponding component on the balance sheet. The statement of retained earnings thus shows the

Exhibit 7-5

Example, Inc.
STATEMENT OF FINANCING ACTIVITIES
FOR 1977

Debt financing	Increase or (decrease)
Notes payable to banks	
Borrowed	$ 50,000
Repaid	(16,908)
Net amount borrowed	33,092
Amounts paid on mortgage payable	(2,000)
Net increase in debt financing	$ 31,092
Equity financing	
Convertible preferred	
Conversion of 300 shares $100 par value 5% convertible preferred for 1,500 shares $10 par value common stock	$(30,000)
Common stock and capital in excess of par value	
Issued 1,500 shares on conversion of 300 shares 5% convertible preferred	30,000
Issued 500 shares for $7,495 cash	7,495
Retained earnings	
Net increase	3,983
Net increase in equity financing	$ 11,478

details of the net change in retained earnings shown on the statement of financing activities.

Activities that involve only changes between components of the stockholders' equity section of the balance sheet, as well as those that affect other sections of the balance sheet, should all be shown on the statement of financing activities. Thus the conversion of Example, Inc.'s, convertible preferred stock into common appears as both a decrease of convertible preferred and an increase in common stock and capital in excess of par value. Similarly, the effect of a stock dividend would also appear on this statement as a decrease in retained earnings and an increase in common stock and capital in excess of par. Although a stock dividend is not a financing activity since it changes no resources or obligations, it is presently accounted for as if it were.

Statement of Investing Activities

A statement of investing activities is the third of the three statements recommended to replace the funds statement. The basic rationale underlying that statement is that long-term investments in assets such as land, plant and equipment, nonmarketable securities, controlled companies, and intangible assets have special significance to financial statement users because they represent relatively inflexible long-term commitments. Changes in a company's holdings of those assets should therefore, be reported.

A statement of investing activities for Example, Inc., is presented in exhibit 7-6. This statement articulates with the other financial statements illustrated in this chapter and chapter 5.

The statement of investing activities should disclose all increases and decreases in long-term investments (including land, plant and equipment, nonmarketable securities, controlled companies, and intangible assets), regardless of how they were acquired or disposed of. The statement of cash receipts and payments, of course, would show investments paid for in cash, and the statement of financing activities would show investments paid for by securities, but only the statement of investing activities would disclose all acquisitions of long-term investments. Decreases in a company's holdings of long-term investments would appear on the statement of cash receipts and payments only if they were sold for cash, and they would almost never appear on the statement of financing activities. They would, however, appear on the statement of investing activities.

Conclusions

The inadequacy of the conventional financial statements as means of disclosing all that needs to be disclosed about the activities of a business enterprise has been recognized for many years. In 1953 A. C. Littleton observed that

> Financial transactions are important and a report of financing stewardship is very much needed, especially when people outside of the enterprise are concerned. Unfortunately, however, no clear and orderly accounting statement for this purpose has evolved that is comparable to the way the income statement fits its purpose. . . .
> It is doubtful if "an application of funds statement" and "an analysis of surplus changes" fully answer the need. The one is too complex in

organization to be understandable; the other is too lacking in organization to be informative.[32]

Exhibit 7-6

Example, Inc.
STATEMENT OF INVESTING ACTIVITIES
FOR YEAR ENDING DECEMBER 31, 1977

Properties	
Land, buildings, and equipment, 12/31/76	$319,101
Plus: Purchases	62,119
	381,220
Less: Cost of properties disposed of	31,595
Land, buildings, and equipment, 12/31/77	$349,625

Although there have been many improvements in financial reporting since Littleton made those comments, a satisfactory way of filling important gaps in disclosure left by the balance sheet and income statement has not evolved. The funds statement has evolved into a statement of changes in financial position, and it has become a required statement, but it is probably less understandable than when Littleton wrote.

The underlying reasons for the failure to develop a satisfactory way of filling the gaps left by the balance sheet and income statement were analyzed in chapter 6. The statement of changes in financial position based on working capital was found to be a dead end, and three replacement statements, a statement of cash receipts and payments, a statement of financing activities, and a statement of investing activities, have, therefore, been recommended in this chapter as replacements for the statement of changes in financial position. The recommended statements do not require the disclosure of significantly more information than is now required to be disclosed. Their principal virtue is that the information would be presented in a clear, understandable way. Statements of changes in financial position have been a contributing factor to the widespread confusion that now exists in the relationships between business activities, profits, and changes in financial position. The proposed statements would not only provide financial statement users with more useful information because it would be more understandable, but these statements would also contribute significantly to the elimination of that confusion.

---

32. A. C. Littleton, *Structure of Accounting Theory*, American Accounting Association Monograph N.S., (Evanston, Ill.: American Accounting Association, 1953), pp. 80-81.

135

8

"Watch Cash Flow"

Three objectives of this study were identified in chapter 1: (1) to increase the awareness of the solvency dimension of financial reporting, (2) to recommend a decision model that identifies the variables relevant in evaluating a company's solvency, and (3) to recommend specific changes in financial reporting practices that would increase the usefulness of financial statements in evaluating a company's solvency.

The specific changes in financial reporting practices recommended in this study are summarized in chapter 1, and are explained and illustrated in chapters 5 and 7. It is not necessary to discuss them further. Some concluding remarks concerning the first two objectives are, however, appropriate at this point.

Solvency Decision Models

As noted in chapter 1, early in this century the problem of evaluating solvency was widely discussed in accounting literature. That discussion, however, was based on a simple decision model. It was a static model based on an assumption that short-term debts are paid with current or "working" assets. The key question asked was whether a company's current assets exceeded its short-term debts by an amount that would enable it to pay those debts even if it were to experience substantial shrinkage in the value of its current assets or, as it was usually stated, whether its working capital "cushion" was adequate.

During the 1950s the relevance of that simple model based on adequacy of working capital began to be questioned in the literature of finance. It was argued that current liabilities are not paid with current assets, that current liabilities do not represent a company's need for cash during the next twelve months, and that current assets do not represent the cash that will be available to meet that need. The model based on adequacy of working capital, in other words, was found to be not just simple, but simplistic. It was what one of its critics called "partial analysis," because it failed to take into account some of the most important variables that determine whether a company will be able to remain solvent.[1]

During the 1930s accountants began to shift their attention from reporting to evaluate solvency to reporting to evaluate profitability. By the 1950s accounting policy makers were concerned almost exclusively with issues in profitability reporting, and the questioning of the model based on adequacy of working capital in the literature of finance went largely unnoticed by them. Today the decision model based on adequacy of working capital still serves as the foundation of the two principal means used to report information on solvency. Current-noncurrent balance sheet classification and funds statements based on working capital changes were both developed during the time when working capital was the center of attention in solvency analysis, and they have been largely unchanged since then. Also, although most writers now preface their remarks about solvency analysis with a caveat to the effect that working capital analysis "does not answer all of the liquidity questions,"[2] those discussions still focus on adequacy of working capital and at least the core of that model, the argument that liabilities are paid with current assets, is still accepted and underlies most discussions of solvency analysis in accounting literature. The authors of one leading intermediate accounting textbook, for example, explain the current ratio as a measure of "the dollars of current assets available to cover each dollar of current debt."[3] The authors of another describe working capital as "the margin of short-term debt paying ability over short-term debt"[4] and note

---

1. James E. Walter, "Determination of Technical Solvency," *Journal of Business*, 30, no. 1 (January, 1957): 32.
2. Donald E. Kieso and Jerry J. Weygandt, *Intermediate Accounting*, 2d ed. (New York: John Wiley, 1977), p. 1021.
3. Kieso and Weygandt, *Intermediate Accounting*, p. 1021.
4. Walter B. Meigs, A. N. Mosich, Charles E. Johnson, and Thomas F. Keller, *Intermediate Accounting*, 3d ed. (New York: McGraw-Hill, 1974), p. 930.

that working capital "may also be viewed as funds available for investment in noncurrent assets or to liquidate noncurrent liabilities."[5]

The first step needed to improve financial reporting for solvency analysis is to replace the simplistic decision model based on adequacy of working capital with a more realistic one that recognizes the variables that are relevant in evaluating a company's solvency. A replacement for the model of solvency evaluation based on adequacy of working capital is described in chapter 2 of this study. A company's expected future cash receipts and payments and its financial flexibility are identified as the relevant variables for evaluating solvency. Assets conventionally classified as current are not important in that model because they can be used to pay short-term debt; they, like all assets, are important only if they normally will, or can in the event of need, result in cash receipts.

The replacement model for solvency evaluation described in this study reflects the way sophisticated users of financial statements evaluate solvency. It was used in this study to examine and evaluate a number of issues in reporting solvency issues and, if used by others, it should provide guidance in examining and evaluating other such issues.

Awareness of Solvency Issues

An improved decision model is an important first step in improving financial reporting for solvency evaluation, but it is not the only step that needs to be taken. As noted in chapter 1, accountants—particularly accountants responsible for setting accounting standards, but also individual accountants and auditors associated with specific financial statements and accounting educators—need to be more aware of the solvency dimension of financial reporting. The discussion in this study of the nature of solvency evaluation, the specific recommendations made for improving solvency information, and the discussion of the reasons underlying those recommendations should all help to increase that awareness. It should not be concluded, however, that all solvency issues have been covered in this study and that the problem would be solved if its specific recommendations are adopted. The problem is deeper than that. Nearly every financial reporting issue faced by both accountants and auditors for specific companies and by accounting standards setters needs to be looked at from the stand-

---

5. Meigs, Mosich, Johnson, and Keller, *Intermediate Accounting*, p. 869.

point of users' needs for solvency information as well as for profitability information. Three areas that require such investigation are given as examples below.

Rising Prices. A period of rising prices creates a cash flow problem and therefore a solvency problem for many companies because increased amounts of cash are needed to replace higher priced assets. To meet that need, either cash receipts and payments from operations have to be adjusted or additional outside financing must be obtained. Information useful in evaluating the magnitude of a company's need for additional cash to replace higher priced assets is, of course, relevant for evaluating solvency under those conditions. Statements of cash receipts and payments, particularly if they are available for several years in which there have been different rates of inflation, and disclosure of the replacement costs of assets held are two types of information that would be useful in estimating a company's need for additional cash to replace assets.

The problem of financial reporting during a period of rising prices is not usually seen from the perspective of solvency. It is typically examined solely from the income measurement point of view. The use of replacement values is supported on the grounds that it provides a superior measure of income, not that it provides information for estimating a company's future cash requirements. Even if the solvency dimension of the problem is recognized, the solution often suggested is to exclude the excess of the replacement value of an asset over its cost from income to obtain a measure known as "distributable" income—a solution that combines and confuses the income measurement and the solvency dimensions of the problem.[6]

Consolidated Statements. The use of consolidated financial statements is another financial reporting issue that needs to be considered from the solvency point of view.

The distinctions between separate legal entities are ignored when consolidated financial statements are prepared; companies within the consolidated group are treated as one economic entity. Legal distinctions between entities, however, are often necessary to

---

6. For discussion of this point see FASB Discussion Memorandum, *An Analysis of Issues Related to Conceptual Framework for Financial Accounting and Reporting: Elements of Financial Statements and Their Measurement*, (Stamford, Conn.: FASB, 1976), chap. 6. See also Paul Rosenfield, "Current Replacement Value Accounting—A Dead End," *Journal of Accountancy*, 140 (September, 1975): 72-73.

evaluate solvency because creditors' rights attach to the separate entities, not to the consolidated entity. From the solvency perspective, a consolidated balance sheet may be misleading because "the pressing liabilities may be in the parent company, but the liquid assets which give promise of meeting these liabilities may be in a subsidiary where they are unavailable to the parent."[7] Similarly, one subsidiary may have adequate cash available, but the "pressing liabilities" may be those of another subsidiary and legal restrictions may prevent transfer of asscts from one subsidiary to another.

Recently the Advisory Committee on Corporate Disclosure to the SEC noted this point and made the following suggestion:

Where there are material blockages to free movements of cash within a consolidated entity (e.g., caused by loan indentures, foreign currency restrictions, or other legal constraints which limit a parent's or a subsidiary's movement of cash to another entity within the consolidated group), separate funds statements might be required for the entity in which the blockage had occurred in order to disclose adequately the significance of this blockage to the ability of the consolidated entity as a whole to meet its dividend, debt service, and other commitments from internally generated cash.[8]

While separate statements of cash receipts and payments for some or all of the companies composing a consolidated entity probably would be useful in the situation described, they are not a complete solution to the problem because balance sheets, too, can be misleading under those conditions. The point in raising this issue, however, is not to recommend a solution, but to demonstrate that consolidated financial statements raise an important issue in the evaluation of solvency that has received little or no attention from accountants. Consolidated financial statements are usually justified by the argument that they are intended to portray the economic substance of parent-subsidiary relationships rather than the legal form of those

---

7. Ted J. Fiflis and Homer Kripke, *Accounting for Business Lawyers*, 2d ed. (St. Paul: West Publishing Co., 1977), p. 604. For a discussion of a recent example in which this issue is raised, see Abraham J. Briloff, "Whose 'Deep Pocket'?" *Barron's*, July 19, 1976, p. 5.
8. U. S., Congress, House, *Report of the Advisory Committee on Corporate Disclosure to the Securities and Exchange Commission*, printed for the use of the House Committee on Interstate and Foreign Commerce, 95th Cong. 1st Sess., Committee Print 95-29, November 3, 1977, p. 505n.

relationships. That argument is specious because a financial statement user concerned with solvency considerations often finds that the legal form of a relationship *determines* its economic substance and, therefore, cannot be ignored. The use of consolidated financial statements, like the problem of financial reporting during periods of changing prices, needs to be looked at from the solvency point of view as well as the income measurement point of view.

Pension Accounting. Pension accounting provides a third example of an issue that needs to be considered in terms of solvency.

A company's obligation to make periodic payments to fund its pension plan often represents a significant cash drain and may be an important consideration in evaluating its solvency. The amount of that obligation cannot be determined by the amount of pension expense reported on its income statement because funding requirements may differ greatly from pension expense reporting requirements.

Current generally accepted accounting principles do not require a company to provide any information about its obligation to provide funding for its pension plan over the next several years. They do not even require it to disclose the amount of its contribution to its pension fund for past periods. APB Opinion no. 18, *Accounting for the Cost of Pension Plans*, is, as its title suggests, concerned almost exclusively with the *cost*, that is, the income effect of pension plans. It ignores their impact on a company's solvency.

Conclusion

Recently, the Advisory Committee on Corporate Disclosure to the SEC recommended that "in evaluating accounting standards, consideration should be given to . . . the adequacy of information useful in assessing the liquidity of the reporting entity."[9] With two minor exceptions[10] that committee did not explain why it believed consideration should be given to the adequacy of that type of information, and it did not elaborate on the type of disclosure needed to assess the liquidity or, as it is called in this study, the solvency of business enterprises. This study explains why increased attention needs to be

---

9. *Report of the Advisory Committee on Corporate Disclosure*, p. 502.
10. See the arguments of that committee for cash flow information quoted in chap. 7 of this study and the argument for separate funds statements quoted earlier in this chapter.

given to that objective. It recommends several changes in reporting practices that would enable financial statement users to better assess or evaluate the solvency of business enterprises, and it points out additional issues in financial reporting that need to be considered from a solvency point of view. With this elaboration, accountants and accounting standards setting bodies are now in a position to begin implementing needed changes in financial reporting for the evaluation of solvency.

Bibliography

Books

ANTON, HECTOR R. *Accounting for the Flow of Funds.* Boston: Houghton Mifflin Co., 1962.
———, and JAEDICKE, ROBERT K. In *Handbook of Modern Accounting.* Edited by Sidney Davidson. New York: McGraw-Hill, 1970.
ARTHUR ANDERSEN & CO. *Accounting and Reporting Problems of the Accounting Profession.* 5th ed. New York: Arthur Andersen & Co., 1976.
BACKER, MORTON. *Financial Reporting for Security Investment and Credit Decisions.* NAA Research Studies in Management Reporting no. 3. New York: National Association of Accountants, 1970.
BECKHART, BENJAMIN HAGGOTT, ed. *Business Loans of American Commercial Banks.* New York: Ronald Press, 1959.
BLOUGH, CARMAN G. *Practical Applications of Accounting Standards.* New York: American Institute of Certified Public Accountants, 1957.
BOGEN, JULES I. *Financial Handbook.* 3d ed. New York: Ronald Press, 1948.
BURNS, THOMAS J., ed. *The Use of Accounting Data in Decision Making,* College of Commerce and Administration Monograph no. AA1. Columbus: Ohio State University, 1967.
COLE, WILLIAM MORSE. *Accounts: Their Construction and Interpretation.* Rev. and enlarged. Boston: Houghton Mifflin, 1915.
DEWING, ARTHUR STONE. *The Financial Policy of Corporations,* 5th ed. Vols. 1 and 2. New York: Ronald Press, 1953.
DONALDSON, GORDON. *Strategy for Financial Mobility.* Boston: Harvard University Press, 1969.
FINNEY, H. A. *Principles of Accounting.* Vol. 1. New York: Prentice-Hall, 1923.

———. *Principles of Accounting, Intermediate.* New York: Prentice-Hall, 1934.

FITZGERALD, A. A., and SCHUMER, L. A. *Classification in Accounting.* Sydney: Butterworths, 1962.

FOULKE, ROY A. *Practical Financial Statement Analysis.* 6th ed. New York: McGraw-Hill, 1968.

———. *The Genesis of the 14 Important Ratios.* New York: Dun and Bradstreet, 1955.

———, and PROCHNOW, HERBERT V. *Practical Bank Credit.* New York: Prentice-Hall, 1939.

GILMAN, STEPHEN. *Accounting Concepts of Profit.* New York: Ronald Press, 1939.

GOODMAN, HORTENSE, and LORENSON, LEONARD. *Illustrations of the Statement of Changes in Financial Position: A Survey of Reporting Under APB Opinion no. 19.* New York: American Institute of Certified Public Accountants, 1974.

GUTHMANN, HARRY G. *Analysis of Financial Statements.* 4th ed. New York: Prentice-Hall, 1953.

HAYAKAWA, S. I. *Language in Thought and Action.* 2d ed. New York: Harcourt, Brace & World, 1964.

HELFERT, ERICH A., ed. *Techniques of Financial Analysis.* Homewood, Ill.: Richard D. Irwin, 1963.

———. In *Financial Analyst's Handbook.* Vol. 1. Edited by Sumner N. Levine. Homewood, Ill.: Dow Jones-Irwin, 1975.

HENDRIKSEN, ELDON S. *Accounting Theory.* 3d ed. Homewood, Ill.: Richard D. Irwin, 1977.

HOLTZ, JAMES NORMAN. *The Financial Concept of Working Capital.* Ph.D. dissertation, University of Michigan, 1962.

HOWARD, BION B., and UPTON, MILLER. *Introduction to Business Finance.* New York: McGraw-Hill, 1953.

INVESTMENT BANKERS ASSOCIATION OF AMERICA. *Fundamentals of Investment Banking.* New York: Prentice-Hall, 1949.

JAEDICKE, ROBERT K., and SPROUSE, ROBERT T. *Accounting Flows: Income, Funds, and Cash.* Englewood Cliffs, N.J.: Prentice-Hall, 1965.

KESTER, ROY B. *Accounting Theory and Practice.* New York: Ronald Press, 1918.

LEV, BARUCH. *Financial Statement Analysis: A New Approach.* Englewood Cliffs, N.J.: Prentice-Hall, 1974.

MASON, PERRY. *"Cash Flow" Analysis and the Funds Statement.* AICPA Accounting Research Study no. 2. New York: American Institute of Certified Public Accountants, 1961.

MAUTZ, R. K. *An Accounting Technique for Reporting Financial Transactions.* University of Illinois, Bureau of Economic and Business Research, Special Bulletin no. 7. Urbana, Ill.: University of Illinois, 1951.

MAY, GEORGE O. *Financial Accounting: A Distillation of Experience.* New York: Macmillan, 1946.

NATIONAL ASSOCIATION OF ACCOUNTANTS. *Cash Flow Analysis for Managerial Control.* NAA Research Report no. 38. New York: National Association of Accountants, 1961.

PARK, COLIN. "Funds Flow." In *Modern Accounting Theory.* Edited by Morton Backer. Englewood Cliffs, N.J.: Prentice-Hall, 1966.

————, and GLADSON, JOHN W. *Working Capital.* New York: Macmillan, 1963.

PATON, W. A. *Advanced Accounting.* New York: Macmillan, 1941.

ROSEN, LAWRENCE S. *A Critical Examination of "Funds" Statement Concepts*, Ph.D. dissertation, University of Washington, 1966.

U.S. CONGRESS. House of Representatives. *Report of the Advisory Committee on Corporate Disclosure to the Securities and Exchange Commission.* Printed for the use of the House Committee on Interstate and Foreign Commerce. 95th Cong. 1st sess. Committee Print 95-29. November 3, 1977.

VATTER, WILLIAM J. *The Fund Theory of Accounting and Its Implications for Financial Reports.* Chicago: University of Chicago Press, 1947.

Journals

ASHBURNE, JIM G. "A Forward Looking Statement of Financial Position." *Accounting Review*, July, 1962.

BARTLEY, GUY. "Letter to the Editor." *Journal of Accountancy*, October, 1925, pp. 311–312.

BEAVER, WILLIAM H. "Alternative Accounting Measures as Predictors of Failure." *Accounting Review*, January, 1968, pp. 113–122.

————. "Financial Ratios as Predictors of Failure." *Empirical Research in Accounting, Selected Studies, 1966.* Supplement to vol. 4, *Journal of Accounting Research*, pp. 77–127.

————, KENNELLY, JOHN W., and VOSS, WILLIAM M. "Predictive Ability as a Criterion for the Evaluation of Accounting Data." *Accounting Review*, October, 1968, pp. 675–683.

BIERMAN, HAROLD, JR. "Measuring Financial Liquidity." *Accounting Review*, October, 1960, pp. 628–632.

BRILOFF, ABRAHAM J. "Whose 'Deep Pocket'?" *Barron's*, July 19, 1976, p. 5.

BLOUGH, CARMAN G. "Classification of Prepaid Expenses as Current Assets." *Robert Morris Associates Bulletin*, February, 1948, pp. 351–353.

———. "Current or Noncurrent, That Is the Question." *Journal of Accountancy*, April, 1954, pp. 484–485.

BRADISH, RICHARD D. "Corporate Reporting and the Financial Analyst." *Accounting Review*, October, 1965, pp. 757–766.

BULLINGTON, ROBERT A. "How Corporate Debt Issues Are Rated." *Financial Executive*, September, 1974, pp. 28–30.

BUZBY, STEPHEN L., and FALK, HAIM. "A New Approach to the Funds Statement." *Journal of Accountancy*, January, 1974, pp. 55–61.

CARSON, A. B. "A 'Source and Application of Funds' Philosophy of Financial Accounting." *Accounting Review*, April, 1949, pp. 159–170.

COLLINS, GEORGE WILLIAM. "An Analysis of Working Capital." *Accounting Review*, October, 1946, pp. 430–431.

"Comments on '"Cash Flow" Analysis and the Funds Statement.'" *Journal of Accountancy*, September, 1962, pp. 63–67.

COOPER, ERNEST. "Chartered Accountants and the Profit Question." *The Accountant*, November 24, 1894, pp. 1033–1043.

CORBIN, DONALD A. "Proposals for Improving Funds Statements." *Accounting Review*, July, 1961, pp. 398–405.

———, and TAUSSIG, RUSSELL. "The AICPA Funds Statement Study," *Journal of Accountancy*, July, 1962, pp. 57–62.

COUGHLAN, JOHN W. "Funds and Income." *NAA Bulletin*, September, 1964, pp. 23–34.

———. "Working Capital and Credit Standing." *Journal of Accountancy*, November, 1960, pp. 44–50.

DICKINSON, W. S. "Method and Arrangement in Accounts." *The Accountant*, February 15, 1902, pp. 188–193.

DILWORTH, RICHARD H. "'Working Capital Revisited." *Robert Morris Associates Bulletin*, May, 1960, pp. 293–296.

DREBIN, ALLAN R. "'Cash Flowitis': Malady or Syndrome?" *Journal of Accounting Research*, Spring, 1964, pp. 25–34.

DUN, L. C. "Working Capital—A Logical Concept." *Australian Accountant*, October, 1969, pp. 461–464.

EL-MOTAAL, M. H. B. ABD. "Working Capital: Its Role in the Short-run Liquidity Policy of Industrial Concerns." *Accounting Research*, 9 (1958): 258–275.

ESQUERRE, PAUL-JOSEPH. "Letter to the Editor." *Journal of Accountancy*, May, 1925, pp. 424–430.
FELDMAN, SAUL. "A Critical Appraisal of the Current Asset Concept." *Accounting Review*, October, 1959, pp. 574–578.
FESS, PHILIP E. "The Working Capital Concept." *Accounting Review*, April, 1966, pp. 266–270.
———. "Improving Working Capital Analysis." *New York CPA*, July, 1967, pp. 506–511.
———, and WEYGANDT, JERRY JO. "Cash Flow Presentations-Trends, Recommendations." *Journal of Accountancy*, August, 1969, pp. 52–59.
FINANCIAL ANALYSTS FEDERATION. "Statement Endorsing the Use of Funds Statements." *Financial Analysts Journal*, May-June, 1964, pp. 13–14.
FINNEY, H. A. "The Statement of Application of Funds." *Journal of Accountancy*, December, 1923, pp. 460–472.
———. "The Statement of Application of Funds: A Reply to Mr. Esquerre." *Journal of Accountancy*, June, 1925, pp. 497–511.
FITZGERALD, A. A. "The Classification of Assets." *Accounting Research*, 1 (1950): 357–372.
FREEMAN, C. E. "Letter to the Editor." *Journal of Accountancy*, October, 1925, pp. 305–311.
GIESE, J. W., and KLAMMER, T. P. "Achieving the Objectives of APB Opinion no. 19." *Journal of Accountancy*, March, 1974, pp. 54–61.
GILMAN, STEPHEN. "Accounting Principles and the Current Classification." *Accounting Review*, April, 1944, pp. 109–116.
GLICKMAN, RICHARD, and STAHL, RICHARD. "The Case of the Misleading Balance Sheet." *Journal of Accountancy*, December, 1968, pp. 68–72.
GOLDBERG, L. "A Note on Current Assets." *Abacus*, September, 1968, pp. 31–45.
GOLDBERG, LOUIS. "The Funds Statement Reconsidered." *Accounting Review*, October, 1951, pp. 485–491.
GOLE, VICTOR L. "Working Capital Ratio—It Needs a Face-Lift." *Australian Accountant*, March, 1954, pp. 90–94.
GREER, HOWARD C. "Structural Fundamentals of Financial Statements." *Accounting Review*, July, 1943, pp. 193–205.
GREGORY, ROBERT H., and WALLACE, EDWARD L. "Solution of Funds Statements Problems—History and Proposed New Method." *Accounting Research*, April, 1952, pp. 99–132.
GYNTHER, MERLE M. "Future Growth Aspects of the Cash Flow Computation." *Accounting Review*, October, 1968, pp. 706–718.

HARNDEN, WILLARD J., and ROSENBAUM, ALLAN S. "Balance Sheet Presentation of Notes Payable." *Colorado CPA Report*, January, 1967, pp. 10–12.
HEATH, LOYD C. "Calculation and Meaning of Cash Flow in Security Analysis." *Financial Analysts Journal*, September-October, 1962, pp. 65–67.
HERRICK, ANSON. "A Review of the Work of the Accounting Procedure Committee." *Journal of Accountancy*, November, 1954, pp. 627–638.
―――. "Current Assets and Liabilities." *Journal of Accountancy*, January, 1944, pp. 48–55.
―――. "What Should Be Included in Current Assets." *Journal of Accountancy*, January, 1932, pp. 51–62.
―――. "Comments by Anson Herrick." *Journal of Accountancy*, November, 1960, pp. 50–52.
HIRSCHMAN, ROBERT W. "A Look at Current Classifications." *Journal of Accountancy*, November, 1967, pp. 54–58.
HORNGREN, CHARLES T. "Increasing the Utility of Financial Statements." *Journal of Accountancy*, July, 1959, pp. 39–46.
HORRIGAN, JAMES O. "Some Empirical Bases of Financial Ratio Analysis." *Accounting Review*, July, 1965, pp. 558–568.
HUMPHREY, FRED L. Letter to the Editor. *Journal of Accountancy*, December, 1925, pp. 464–468.
HUNT, PEARSON. "Funds Position: Keystone in Financial Planning." *Harvard Business Review*, May-June, 1975, pp. 106–115.
JOHNSON, CRAIG. "Ratio Analysis and the Prediction of Firm Failure." *Journal of Finance*, December, 1970, pp. 1166–1168.
KÄFER, KARL, and ZIMMERMAN, V. K. "Notes on the Evolution of the Statement of Sources and Applications of Funds." *International Journal of Accounting*, Spring, 1967, pp. 89–121.
KEMPNER, JACK J. "A New Look at the Classification of Inventories." *Accounting Review*, April, 1960, pp. 264–271.
KOHLER, E. L. "Tendencies in Balance Sheet Construction." *Accounting Review*, December, 1926, pp. 1–11.
KRIPKE, HOMER. "A Search for a Meaningful Securities Disclosure Policy." *Business Lawyer*, November, 1975, pp. 293–317.
LAERI, J. HOWARD. "The Audit Gap." *Journal of Accountancy*, March, 1966, pp. 57–59.
LEACH, CAMPBELL W. "A New Look at Working Capital." *Journal of Accountancy*, March, 1962, pp. 237–243.
LEMKE, KENNETH W. "The Evaluation of Liquidity: An Analytical Study." *Journal of Accounting Research*, Spring, 1970, pp. 47–77.

Levy, Harry. "Nature and Significance of Working Capital." *Australian Accountant*, September, 1959, pp. 517–525.

Littleton, A. C. "High Standards of Accounting." *Journal of Accountancy*, August, 1938, pp. 99–104.

―――――. "The 2-to-1 Ratio Analyzed." *Certified Public Accountant*, August, 1926, pp. 244–246.

Mauriello, Joseph A. "Realization as the Basis of Asset Classification and Measurement." *Accounting Review*, January, 1963.

―――――. "The All-Inclusive Statement of Funds." *Accounting Review*, April, 1964, pp. 347–357.

―――――. "The Working Capital Concept—A Restatement." *Accounting Review*, January, 1962, pp. 39–43.

Moonitz, Maurice. "Inventories and the Statement of Funds." *Accounting Review*, July, 1943, pp. 262–266.

Mueller, F. W., Jr. "Corporate Working Capital and Liquidity." *Journal of Business*, July, 1953, pp. 157–172.

Murray, Roger F. "The Penn Central Debacle: Lessons for Financial Analysis." *Journal of Finance*, May, 1971, pp. 327–332.

Nelson, Edward G. "A Brief Study of Balance Sheets." *Accounting Review*, October, 1947, pp. 341–352.

"Not to Mislead the Public." *Journal of Accountancy*, July, 1964, pp. 23–24.

Park, Colin. "Working Capital and the Operating Cycle." *Accounting Review*, July, 1951, pp. 299–307.

Paton, William A. "The 'Cash Flow' Illusion." *Accounting Review*, April, 1963, pp. 243–251.

Pautler, Hebert A. "An All-Purpose Funds Statement—Basis and Development." *NAA Bulletin*, February, 1963, pp. 3–17.

―――――. "Operating Uses for Funds Data." *NAA Bulletin*, June, 1963, pp. 15–28.

Peirson, C. G. "Fund Flows and Price Changes." *Australian Accountant*, July, 1968, pp. 402–406.

Peloubet, Maurice E. "Valuation of Normal Stocks at Fixed Prices." *Accountant*, November 23, 1929, pp. 650–656.

―――――. "Current Assets and the Going Concern." *Journal of Accountancy*, July, 1928, pp. 18–22.

―――――. "Special Problems in Accounting for Capital Assets." *Journal of Accountancy*, March, 1936, pp. 185–198.

―――――. Letter to the Editor on "Classification of Assets." *Journal of Accountancy*, October, 1932, pp. 309–310.

PERRY, JAMES E. "Analyzing the Borrower's Situation." *Journal of Accountancy*, October, 1977, pp. 101–103. Reprinted from *Banking*, June, 1977.

"Prepaid Expenses as Current Assets." *Journal of Accountancy*, April, 1948, pp. 273–274.

PROCHNOW, HERBERT V. "Bank Liquidity and the New Doctrine of Anticipated Income." *Journal of Finance*, December, 1949, pp. 298–314.

ROBERTS, AUBREY C., and GABHART, DAVID R. L. "Statement of Funds: A Glimpse of the Future?" *Journal of Accountancy*, April, 1972, pp. 54–59.

ROSE, HAROLD. "Sources and Uses: A British View." *Journal of Accounting Research*, Autumn, 1964, pp. 137–146.

ROSEN, L. S., and DECOSTER, DON T. "'Funds' Statements: An Historical Perspective." *Accounting Review*, January, 1969, pp. 124–136.

ROSENFIELD, PAUL. "Current Replacement Value Accounting—A Dead End." *Journal of Accountancy*, September, 1975, pp. 63–73.

ROSS, HOWARD I. "Some Questions About Working Capital." *Canadian Chartered Accountant*, April, 1955, pp. 227–230.

SAVOIE, LEONARD M. "Including the Funds Statement in Corporate Annual Reports." *Price Waterhouse Review*, Autumn, 1964, pp. 33–35.

SEIDMAN, J. S. Letter to the Editor. *Journal of Accountancy*, June, 1961, p. 31.

SMITH, WILLIAM C. "Dividends and Capital." *Accountant*, July 18, 1903, pp. 933–938.

SORTER, G. H., and BENSTON, GEORGE. "Appraising the Defensive Position of a Firm: The Internal Measure." *Accounting Review*, October, 1960, pp. 633–640.

SPILLER, EARL A., and VIRGIL, ROBERT L. "Effectiveness of APB Opinion no. 19 in Improving Funds Reporting." *Journal of Accounting Research*, Spring, 1974, pp. 112–142.

STAMP, EDWARD. "'A Note on Current Assets': A Comment." *Abacus*, December, 1965, p. 188–189.

STAUBUS, GEORGE J. "Alternative Asset Flow Concepts." *Accounting Review*, July, 1966, pp. 397–412.

STOREY, REED K. "Cash Movements and Periodic Income Determination." *Accounting Review*, July, 1960, pp. 449–454.

VATTER, WILLIAM J. "A Direct Method for the Preparation of Fund Statements." *Journal of Accountancy*, April, 1944, pp. 479–489.

———. "Misconceptions About Depreciation." *American Association of Hospital Accountants*, February, 1960, pp. 12–16.

———. "Operating Confusion: Two Reports or One." *Journal of Business*, July, 1963, pp. 290–301.

WALKER, GEORGE T. "Limitations of the Statement of Funds Applied and Provided." *Journal of Accountancy*, April, 1941, pp. 342–345.

WALTER, JAMES E. "Determination of Technical Solvency." *Journal of Business*, January, 1957, pp. 30–43.

WINBORNE, MARILYN G. "The Operating Cycle Concept." *Accounting Review*, July, 1964, pp. 622–626.

WRIGHT, F. K. "An Examination of the Working Capital Ratio." *Australian Accountant*, March, 1956, pp. 101–107.